The R Rules

For middle and high school students

A guide for teens to identify and build resources

The R Rules: A guide for teens to identify and build resources. Revised Edition 2015
Elizabeth W. Souther
Contributing author: Ruby K. Payne
269 pp.
Bibliography pp. 257–263

ISBN 13: 978-1-938248-40-5

Copyright 2008. Revised 2015 by aha! Process, Inc.
Published by aha! Process, Inc.

All rights reserved. Printed in the United States of America. No part of this book may be reproduced in any manner whatsoever without written permission, except in the case of brief quotations embedded in critical articles and reviews. For information, contact:

aha! Process, Inc.
P.O. Box 727
Highlands, TX 77562-0727
(800) 424-9484 or (281) 426-5300
Fax: (281) 426-5600
Website: http://www.ahaprocess.com

Edited by Jesse Conrad
Book design by Betti Souther
Illustrations by Suzanne Howard
Cover design by ArtLink

"Beaver Cartoon" by Tim Lucas used by permission of Tim Lucas.
Career Clusters icons are being used with permission of the States' Career Clusters Initiative, 2007, www.careerclusters.org.

"Career Survey," as adapted from Career Partnership, used with permission from Marie Schumacher, San Juan College, Farmington, New Mexico, schumacherma@sanjuancollege.edu.

"Categories of Instructional Strategies That Affect Student Achievement" (figure 1.3) from *Classroom Instruction That Works: Research-Based Strategies for Increasing Student Achievement* by Marzano, Pickering, and Pollock © 2001. Reprinted by permission of McREL.

Excerpt from preface to *Merriam-Webster's Encyclopedia of Literature* © 1995 used with permission of the publisher, Merriam-Webster Inc. (www.Merriam-Webster.com).

"Introduction" by Lee Jenkins reprinted with permission from *Permission to Forget,* ASQ Quality Press © 2005 American Society for Quality.

"Rewrite this story using different language" adapted from McREL workshop handouts presented by Diane Paynter at Apache Elementary School, Farmington, New Mexico, 2005. Used with permission of McREL.

"Tools Section" developed by Glenda Brown and Betti Souther. Used with permission of Glenda Brown. "Word, Term, or Concept" table adapted with permission from Diane Paynter, author of *For the Love of Words*.

The R Rules

REVISED EDITION

For middle and high school students

A guide for teens to identify and build resources

Elizabeth W. Souther
Contributing Author: Ruby K. Payne, Ph.D.

Table of Contents

Introduction	1
Chapter 1—Road Trip	25
Chapter 2—Relevance	51
Chapter 3—Resources	73
Chapter 4—Rules	97
Chapter 5—Realities	111
Chapter 6—Register	145
Chapter 7—Relationships	161
Chapter 8—Review	175
Chapter 9—Response	193
Chapter 10—Reframe	205
Chapter 11—Road Ready	223
Appendix	239
Bibliography	257

The R Rules

1. Rules − Relationships = Rebellion
"Rules without relationships breed rebellion."
—Grant East

2. Rules + Rigor + Relationship = Resources, Results, Respect
To get resources, results, and respect, understand the rules, rigor, and relationships.

3. Resources = Choices
More Resources = More Choices

These three "r rules" are the foundation of all activities and information presented in this course. Use *The R Rules* to increase awareness about yourself and your community, identify resources, and build skills that will help you navigate and succeed in the complex environments of the 21st century.

During this class you will create and use education and career plans to turn your goals and dreams into realities. Working with peers, facilitators, and community members, you will complete projects; develop management, organization, and leadership skills; and contribute and make a difference.

In *The R Rules,* life is like a card game. Everyone gets a hand. We all get good hands, and we all get bad hands. While you can't control the cards you were dealt, you can control how you play them. Use *The R Rules* to learn about yourself, build resources, and win more often in the game of life.

Welcome to The R Rules ...

The R Rules

R Rules Introduction
The "R Rules" Formulas, Future Pictures, Personal Planner, Life Is Like a Card Game, Hope

Chapter 1 – Road Trip
Begin with the End in Mind: Rules, Rigor, Processes, and Procedures; Mission Statements, Goal Setting, Action Plans, and Project Management

Chapter 2 – Relevance
Situational Awareness, Relevance, Prioritizing, Patterns, Voice

Chapter 3 – Resources
Ten Resources, Social Capital, Community Resource Project, 21st Century Skills

Chapter 4 – Rules
Rules – Written and Unwritten – at Home, Work, School; Patterns, Economic Class

Chapter 5 – Realities
Exploration and Planning: Financial, College, Workforce, and Career

Chapter 6 – Register
Language and Vocabulary for Voice, Communication, Negotiation

Chapter 7 – Relationships
Relationships: Personal, Interpersonal, and Learning; Resilience, Relationship Bank Account

Chapter 8 – Review
Critical and Creative Thinking, Paradigms, Perspectives, Role Models, Self-Talk

Chapter 9 – Response
Responses for Results, Resilience, Resources

Chapter 10 – Reframe
Translating and Applying Information; Reframing Resources and Future Pictures

Chapter 11 – Road Ready
Citizenship, Leadership, Transitions for College, Work, and Careers

Introduction—Learning Objectives

What?	Why?	How?
I. The R Rules	Explain the foundation and purpose of *The R Rules*.	Use mental models to define and share understanding.
II. Life Is Like a Card Game	We are all dealt a hand in the game of life. You cannot control the cards you are dealt, but you can control how you play them.	Use a card game to create a mental model of life for yourself and this class; identify expectations and resources.
III. Registers of Language	All languages have five registers. There are rules about when and where each register is used.	Use registers to communicate, negotiate, and achieve in different environments.
IV. Vocabulary Six-Step Process	Words are tools the mind uses to communicate, complete tasks, and share dreams and ideas.	Use the six-step process to build language and vocabulary for school, work, and life.
V. Larissa's Story	Use the card game to develop a mental model for an individual.	Use Larissa's story to develop her hand, see options, and plan.
VI. Relationships	Relationships can be a driver and a barrier to reaching goals. Individuals often must change how they spend time to achieve.	Understand how relationships and patterns are relevant to learning, reaching personal goals, future pictures, and achievement.
VII. A Future Picture	If you can see it, you can be it! Using a future picture can inspire and guide you in reaching goals.	Use future pictures as mental models to translate ideas into actions, plan, and reach goals.
VIII. Personal Planners	Personal planners reflect *you!* Use to store, organize, and manage information; reach personal goals; and contribute.	Create and use R Rules Personal Planners and R Rules Professional Portfolios for school, college, jobs, careers, and life.
IX. What Do You Value?	Core values are relevant to behaviors and choices.	Explore core values, develop resources, and make choices.
X. Hope R^u Reflection	Message from the author. Hope motivates. Hope and reflection are important resources.	Review and use to further your vision. Use reflection to increase awareness, apply information.
XI. Check Your Hand	Mental models help identify current pictures and plan for future pictures.	Create a personal mental model using the card game to identify and build resources.
XII. R Rules Raffiti	Personal space for you to write, create, reflect in YOUR planner.	Create, doodle, and record what is important to you. Have fun!
XIII. R Rules Rubric	R Rules rubrics are tools to self-assess, sort, and use information.	Assess learning; use information to build resources to reach goals.
XIV. Definitions, Symbols, Mental Models, and Tools	Definitions of words, symbols, mental models, and tools.	Use to increase knowledge and resources.
Check items to be filed in your R Rules Personal Planner.		

I. The R Rules

1. Rules – Relationships = Rebellion
   "Rules without relationships breed rebellion."
   –Grant East

2. Rules + Rigor + Relationship = Resources, Results, Respect
   To get resources, results, and respect—understand the rules, rigor, and relationships.

3. Resources = Choices
   More Resources = More Choices

In *The R Rules* ...

II.  *Life is like a card game ...*
Everyone gets a set of cards.
You can't control the cards you get.
You can decide how to play them.

Check the cards in your hand.
    Sometimes other players have the same cards you were dealt.
    Sometimes the cards are different.

We all ...
    Have hopes and fears, goals and dreams.
    Face unique challenges and situations.
    Use the resources that are available.
    Are problem solvers.

We all ...
1. Live in a particular region or part of a country.
2. Belong to a group or groups based on cultural heritage.
3. Face the possibility of illness or disability.
4. Have intelligence and an education—formal and/or informal.
5. Will experience the effects of aging.
6. Deal with various expectations related to gender.
7. Have an economic reality and are members of an economic class.
8. Use the rules and patterns we know.
9. Have a variety of resources—external and internal.
10. Use languages to communicate and negotiate.

We are all different. We are all alike.

II. Life is like a card game ...
Upon completion of The R Rules, you will be able to:

... explain three r rules.

... develop current and future pictures and set goals.

... use an R Rules Personal Planner to monitor progress.

... create and use mental models.

... achieve and contribute as a member of a team and learning community.

... recognize, analyze, and apply patterns.

... identify, develop, and apply resources to contribute and achieve.

... use resources in different systems, environments, and situations.

... increase financial literacy; access systems that support future pictures.

... develop an R Rules Professional Portfolio and education and employment plans.

... use language to communicate, negotiate, and have a voice.

... explain the relevance of relationships.

... use critical and creative thinking.

... solve problems and make informed decisions.

... demonstrate organization, management, and leadership skills.

... contribute as a citizen in local and global communities.

II. Life is like a card game...
   Identify expectations and goals for this class.

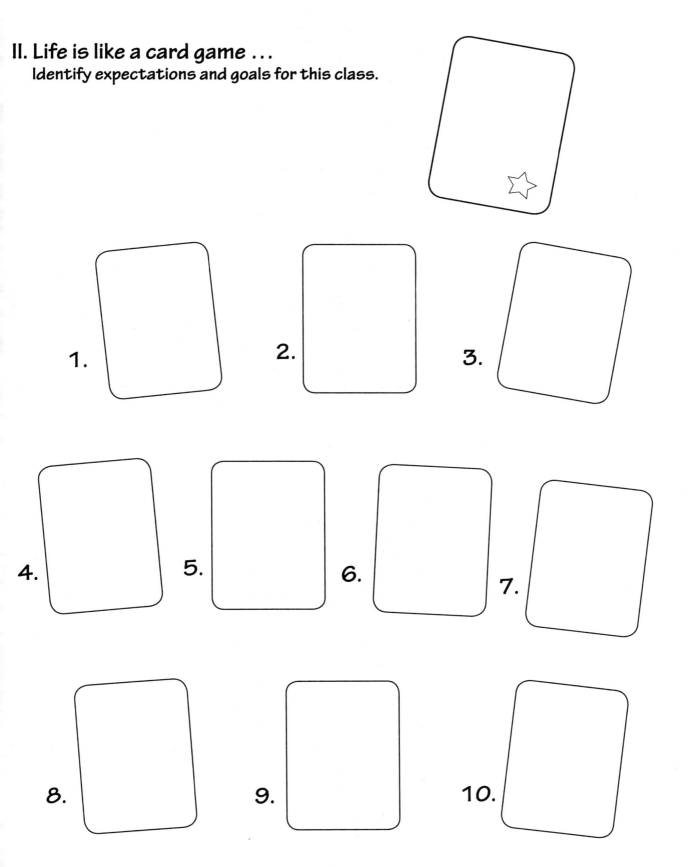

III. Registers of Language

One Register: OK!
Two Registers: GO AWAY!

Register	Explanation
	Frozen – Language that is always the same. *Examples: Pledge of Allegiance, Lord's Prayer, ceremonies, Constitution, brand names, Miranda warning, Gettysburg Address, "please," "thank you," "you are welcome"*
	Formal – Standard sentence syntax and word choice of school and work. Complete sentences and specific word choices. *Examples: textbooks, newspapers, applications, technical manuals, lectures, scholarships, job interviews*
	Consultative – Formal register when used in conversation. Discourse not quite as direct as formal register. Mix of formal and casual. *Examples: explanation of repairs to a vehicle, consultation, conferences, collaboration, classroom instruction*
	Casual – Language between friends. Characterized by a 400- to 800-word vocabulary. Word choice general and not specific. Conversation dependent on nonverbal assists. Sentence syntax often incomplete. *Examples: they, it, that way, hey, yo, huh, yup, lol, j/k, use of hands to indicate a direction*
	Intimate – Language of twins and personal relationships. Communication specific to participants. Language of discipline referrals and sexual harassment. Shared, exclusive language and meanings. *Examples: a look, a shrug, "she's a mable," "the gizzle," "the whatchamacallit"*

Registers of language from the work of M. Joos and R. Payne.

Example of syntax: Adjective is before a noun.
Example of discourse: Speaker gets right to the point.

III. Registers of Language

Register	Explanation
	Frozen
	Formal
	Consultative
	Casual
	Intimate

IV. Vocabulary Six-Step Process

WORDS are the tools we use to share ideas, knowledge, hopes, and dreams.

1. The Word or Term	
2. Definition	**3. In Your Words**
textbook test technical term	written in your own words
4. Mental Model	**5. Connections**
	notes synonym or antonym
6. Home Language:	

Vocabulary process adapted and used with permission from the work of Diane Paynter.

1. United States of America	
2. Definition	**3. In Your Words**
4. Mental Model	**5. Connections**
6. Home Language:	

GAME DAYS!

IV. Vocabulary

V. Larissa's Story
Life Is Like a Card Game

Read Larissa's story on page 13 and use the information to identify Larissa's goal and the cards in her hand.

 GOAL

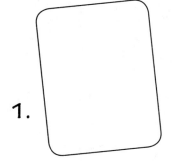 1.

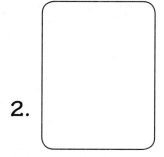 2.

 3.

4.

5.

6.

7.

8.

9.

10.

V. Larissa's Story

Larissa is in the 10th grade. She likes school and learning. She has a 3.8 GPA and plans to attend college and earn a degree after high school graduation. Larissa has completed one advanced placement course and will complete at least one more this school year. She likes science, participated in the science fair, is on the debate team, and won an award in a fashion design contest. Last year she completed a tour of the local community college and is interested in learning about the classes and programs available there.

Larissa is 15 years of age, identifies as female, and states her cultural heritage is Hispanic. Larissa lives in a small town in northern New Mexico. The community is rural and has limited public transportation. The population is around 45,000, but on the weekends stores and restaurants fill with people who travel from surrounding areas to shop and access services not offered in their smaller communities. Employment in the area is related to oil and gas production, farming and agriculture, retail stores, government, and education.

Larissa and her family—her grandmother, father, mother, two brothers, and sister—have lived in the area for the past two years. Larissa's mother has a medical condition that requires special care. Larissa's grandmother recently moved in with the family, and Larissa is grateful for the help she provides, particularly caring for her mother and baby sister. Larissa is bilingual and often translates for her grandmother and mother when a call to the school or doctor's office is necessary.

Larissa's father has worked for the same company for the past two years, but the work is not always steady. Schedules vary from week to week. Her father is a skilled mason and sometimes picks up a side job to earn extra money. Larissa and her brothers participate in the free and reduced lunch program at school.

The family rents a three-bedroom house near the elementary school Larissa's brothers attend. Her brothers are able to walk to school. In order to get to the high school, Larissa rides the school bus. Occasionally Tom, Larissa's boyfriend, drives his car to school, and Larissa rides with him. Larissa and Tom have been dating for several months.

Larissa's family has lived in their current neighborhood for less than a year. Though the new house is bigger, Larissa wishes they were back in their old neighborhood. Larissa had lots of friends, and the neighborhood families were close, shared celebrations and holidays together. Larissa sees some of her friends at the church in the old neighborhood where she and her family attend regularly. She has worked on several community and service projects with the church youth group.

We all ...
1. Live in a particular region or part of a country.
2. Belong to a group or groups based on cultural heritage.
3. Face the possibility of illness or disability.
4. Have intelligence and an education—formal and/or informal.
5. Will experience the effects of aging.
6. Deal with various expectations related to gender.
7. Have an economic reality and are members of an economic class.
8. Use the rules and patterns we know.
9. Have a variety of resources—external and internal.
10. Use languages to communicate and negotiate.

VI. Relationships

Relationships:
- *Can be a driver to help reach a goal.*
- *Can be a roadblock.*

Identify relationships and discuss:
- *Drivers and roadblocks for Larissa.*
- *Drivers and roadblocks for this course.*
- *Options and strategies.*

Goal Mobile

Why?

Check your cards for relationships.

Sometimes individuals must change how they spend their time in order to reach a goal.

*Review your cards.
What cards will you add?
What cards will you discard?*

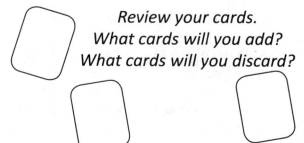

VII. A Future Picture
What do you want to DO, BE, or HAVE?
Create a picture in your mind—a mental model—of the future you want ...
"A FUTURE PICTURE"
Sketch your future picture below.

VIII. Personal Planners

Personal planners reflect who you are and what your future picture looks like. A personal planner is a three-ring binder (different than this workbook) that is created completely by you! It's a way of putting onto paper your goals and dreams so you can express yourself and share information with others to build resources and achieve your future picture.

Your personal planner should:
1. Represent who you are. It belongs to you; make it yours.
2. Help you stay organized and create a safe place for your work.
3. Be organized by section. You keep a list of content for each section so you know where you put things!
4. Contain key information relevant to your personal plan and future picture in each section.

You will create and use seven sections to organize your work and file information. They are:

1. **Personal**
2. **Education**
3. **College**
4. **Career**
5. **Leadership**
6. **Tools**
7. **Units**

Use this graphic as a mental model to remind you about items that will be added to your personal planner. Discuss in class which documents you should include in your personal planner and where they might be filed.

Be prepared to share. Time is scheduled into the regular school day for reviews and updating your planner. This is done using progress checks, rubrics, discussions with peers, and conferences with your instructor to share information and use feedback. Students also use planners to lead conferences with parents or family and develop professional portfolios that are used for college and job interviews.

Create an R Rules Personal Planner using materials and procedures, as directed.
Create a *cover* for *your* planner using text, photos, quotations, and illustrations that represent *you*.

IX. What *do* you value?
What is important to you?

Core Values

_____
_____
_____
_____

www.values.com/pass-it-on-downloads

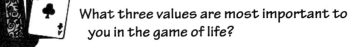 What three values are most important to you in the game of life?

X. Hope

I hope The R Rules *will help you learn about yourself,
about who you are and who you want to be.*

*I hope you are inspired to keep learning,
to operate from a place of hope
rather than a place of resignation.*

*I hope you will see possibilities
where you once accepted limits.
I hope you will ask why and then why not.*

*I hope you will share what you learn with others
so they too will have choices.*

*I hope you will not play small.
I hope that you will develop and
share your unique talents and skills,
and by doing so you will
give others permission to do the same.*

*I hope you will use your mind as a tool
to invent and discover.*

*I hope you will use your mind as a weapon
to fight fear and injustice.*

*I hope you will use your mind as a resource to create
the future we all hope to live in.*

*I hope you will have courage to take new roads.
I hope you will follow your dreams.
I hope.*

—Betti Souther

X. Hope

R^u = R Rules to the power of YOU

What do you hope to do?

What will you change?

What limits do you accept? Why? Are there other options?

What are your unique talents and skills?

Who encourages you? Who do you encourage?

What would you discover? Invent?

What injustice will you address?

What fear will you fight?

What would the world you want to live in be like?

What or who does courage look like?

What is your dream? What do you hope for?

How will you turn your hopes and dreams into a reality?

XI. Life is like a card game...
Check your hand.
Write your goal in the card on the left.
List information about yourself in each of the cards below.
Use the information to decide how to play the cards in your hand.

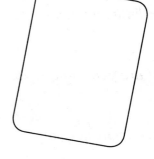

1. 2. 3.

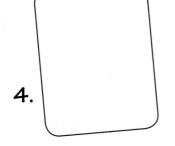

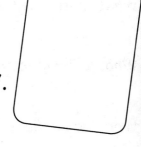

4. 5. 6. 7.

8. 9. 10.

XII. R Rules Raffiti
Use raffiti pages to write notes, reflect,
and EXPRESS your creativity …

I DARE YOU —
Dream BIG!

Dreams are travels for the soul.
If my dream came true, I would …

XIII. R Rules Rubric for Introduction

1. Three R Rules
2. Life Is Like a Card Game
3. Registers of Language
4. Vocabulary Process
5. Larissa's Story
6. Relationships
7. Future Picture
8. Personal Planner
9. Core Values
10. Hope
11. R Rules Raffiti, Rubric, Mental Models, Definitions, Tools

4.0	I understand the chapter and can explain the concepts I learned to others. What I learned is important and can be used in the following ways:
3.0	I understand the chapter and do not have any questions about the concepts. What I learned is important because:
2.0	I understand parts of this chapter. I still don't understand and have questions about:
1.0	I still need help to understand the basic concepts of this chapter. Specifically about:
How I will use what I learned in this chapter:	

Rubric by K. Dixon

XIV. Introduction Definitions, Symbols, Mental Models, Tools

Definitions

Analogy: (example) My life is as busy as an eight-lane superhighway at rush hour.

Core values: The values and foundation that guide our personal choices and how we work and interact with each other to accomplish our goals.

Discourse pattern: How ideas are arranged in language.

Heritage: Something that comes or belongs to you by reason of birth, inheritance, or tradition.

Mental model: How the mind stores information and ideas—in a picture, a story, or an analo Mental models are used to share understanding and clarify meaning. Mental models show the purpose, pattern, structure, or process.

Negotiation: Conversation to reach an agreement, understanding, or outcome.

Pattern: Events, behaviors, forms, or characteristics that repeat—that occur over and over again.

Process: A set of steps or actions to reach an outcome.

Resources: Anything available to a person that can be used to assist, support, or help.

Rigor: The requirements or set of standards used to determine achievement or success.

Syntax: The order of formal language, such as an adjective placed before a noun in a sentence.

Symbols and Mental Models

Check or file in your personal planner

Discussion

Hope and resources

Reflection, analyzing, and using information

Tools

XIV. Introduction Definitions, Symbols, Mental Models, Tools

Tools

Force Field

Tool to identify factors that drive or support an effort and factors that work against the effort or act as barriers.

Step 1: Write the topic, situation, or goal.
Step 2: List the factors driving or supporting reaching the goal.
Step 3: List the factors that are or will be barriers to reaching the goal.
Step 4: Identify factors that will help reach the goal and prioritize them.
Step 5: Prioritize the barriers.
Step 6: Develop a plan to eliminate barriers. Use drivers to reach the goal.

Topic:

Drivers ⟶	⟵ Barriers
1.	1.
2.	2.
3.	3.
4.	4.
5.	5.
6.	6.

Chapter 1 Road Trip—Learning Objectives

What?	Why?	How?
I. Begin with the End in Mind	Knowing where you want to go can assist in planning, choices, and decision making.	Use your future picture to plan, monitor progress, guide choices, and make revisions.
II. Time Maps	Understand past, present, and future to see strengths and plan.	Use a time map to see patterns and develop resources.
III. Tools to See Patterns and Manage	Tools provide a format and process to analyze, use, and revise information.	Apply various tools to see patterns and relationships. Plan and manage to reach goals.
IV. Rules and Rigor	Begin with the end in mind by understanding the rules, rigor, and relationships of this class.	Understand syllabus, rules, policies, requirements, and processes of class and school.
V. Class Mission Statement	Mission statements tell why a group exists, what they are going to do, and how.	Develop and use mission statements to inform and clarify purpose, expectations, and behaviors.
VI. Rubrics	Rubrics state the expectations and define standards to achieve and contribute.	Create and use a rubric to identify and agree on the behaviors in your classroom.
VII. SMART Goals and Action Plans	Writing a goal requires specific information, measures, actions, results, and timelines. Achieving a goal requires planned actions.	Use SMART goals and action plans to set goals, organize, manage, and achieve goals.
VIII. Planning Backwards	To complete a task or reach a goal, begin with the end or goal, and plan backwards.	Use backwards planning to identify outcomes, organize, plan, and manage time.
IX. Teamwork	Teamwork is a resource. Processes, resources, and skills are needed.	Identify drivers and barriers; develop resources to work and achieve as a member of a team.
X. Project Management	Life, school, and work all require the ability to develop, manage, and complete projects and leadership skills.	Develop, manage, and complete projects that will make a positive difference for you and your community.
XI. Raffiti, Rubric, Resources	To provide clarification of information, mental models, and tools.	Use to increase knowledge, resources, and vocabulary; assess learning and apply information.
Check items to be filed in your R Rules Personal Planner.		

In Alice's Adventures in Wonderland, *Alice asked the Cheshire Cat which way she ought to go.*

"That depends a great deal on where you want to get to," said the cat.

When Alice said, "I don't much care where ..."

The cat replied, "Then it doesn't matter which way you go."

"... as long as I get SOMEWHERE," Alice added.

"Oh, you're sure to do that," said the cat, "if you only walk long enough."

Chapter 1—Road Trip
I. Begin with the End in Mind

Stephen Covey says, "All physical creation must first be preceded by mental creation."

As part of developing your future picture, you first created a picture in your mind—a mental creation. This chapter is about translating those mental creations—your thoughts, ideas, and dreams—into plans and actions to make them a reality. Once you have an end in mind—a future picture—brainstorm to determine how you will make it a reality. Ask what, why, how, where, when, and who to translate mental into physical. Your mind is a tool, a weapon, and a resource.

What do you want to do?
Why?
How will you get there?
When will you start?
Where do you want to "get to?"
Who would you like to meet along the way?

Discussion

Life is a road trip, and whether you travel on back roads or superhighways, getting where you want to go will require planning, organization, and management skills. Use information about tools and processes in this chapter to navigate different systems and environments. Use your planner to stay focused on who you are, where you want to go, and to translate dreams and goals into actions and realities.

II. Time Maps

We generally share memories and think about events in a random order based on their emotional importance rather than in the order they actually took place.

Use the chart below to create a "time map" of your life showing the past, present, and future. Each square represents one year. Beginning with Square 1, write the year you were born. Then write the following year in Square 2, and so on through 30. For each year, write a word or sketch an image that represents an important or memorable event that occurred during that year: a move, a birth, marriage, graduation, a new friend, your 18th birthday, etc.

In the squares for years beyond your current age, write or sketch what you want or hope will occur. This is your future story.

1 ____	2 ____	3 ____	4 ____	5 ____
6 ____	7 ____	8 ____	9 ____	10 ____
11 ____	12 ____	13 ____	14 ____	15 ____
16 ____	17 ____	18 ____	19 ____	20 ____
21 ____	22 ____	23 ____	24 ____	25 ____
26 ____	27 ____	28 ____	29 ____	30 ____

What do you do daily, weekly, monthly, every year?
Look for patterns. Identify "momentum" and "milestone" years.
What events or people helped you develop strengths and talents?
What do you look forward to? What traditions do you celebrate or share?
Look at your future picture.
Use information here to see patterns, then predict and plan.
Journal activity—My Future Story

II. Time Maps

A calendar is a time map. Use the one below to plan and manage your year. Start by listing dates that are important to you. Examples: birth dates of people you care about, holidays, vacation time, appointments, etc. File a copy of your schedules and school calendar in your personal planner.

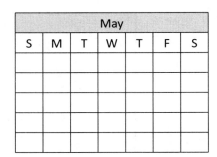

III. Tools to See Patterns and Manage

1. MONITOR YOUR PROGRESS and USE DATA

- 🕐 Schedule time each week to check grades, attendance, and progress reports.
- ✋ Conference with your instructor, peers, and mentors.
- ✋ Use feedback from others, self-checks, and data to revise and build resources and reach goals.
- 📁 File reports and data in your planner.
- 📁 Update and revise regularly.

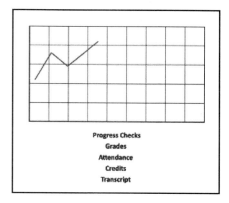

Rules – Relationships = Rework
To get resources, results and respect—
understand rules, rigor, and relationships.

True or False?
"Comprehension changes when data is charted."
–Will Daggett

Obtain, review, and file in your planner:
A copy of your four-year plan
A copy of your program of study
A copy of your transcript
A copy of a blank transcript

If you have questions about any of your personal information, talk to your instructor and follow policies and procedures. Make an appointment with your counselor or school registrar. Take your planner and a copy of your transcript or data to the appointment. Following the appointment, write a brief summary and file in your planner. Include the date, time, who you talked with, information you covered, outcomes, follow-up, and next steps, etc. Update personal information and maintain in your planner.

Appointments 101 ...
Show the process to make an appointment below.

III. Tools to See Patterns and Manage

2. KEEP, START, STOP
Check your future picture. Check the cards in your hand.
What cards will you keep, discard, or draw?
Ask what is working and helping you reach your goals—what you will keep doing?
What is getting in the way or not helping you—what you will stop doing?
What can you do that would help reach goals or improve—what will you start doing?

Keep	Start	Stop

3. FORCE FIELD ANALYSIS
List drivers.
List roadblocks.
Make a plan.

IV. Rules and Rigor

Begin with the End in Mind for This Class ...
Rules, Rigor, Relationships = Resources, Results, Respect
Ask What, Why, How, Where, When, Who

What: Syllabus, learning goals, requirements, expectations, projects, and vocabulary.

Why: Credit for graduation or college; relevance to program of study, future picture, and goals.

Where: Location of classroom, lab, field trips, seat, location of resources and supplies.

When: Day, time, length, start and end dates, assignment dates, and progress checks.

Who: Instructors, assistants, peers, teams, and speakers.

How: Rules, classroom procedures, policies, and processes; grading system and rubrics; progress checks and conferencing; class mission, purpose, and guiding principles.

V. Create a Class Mission Statement

A mission statement tells why a group exists and what the group is going to do.
Mission statements are used by individuals and groups to communicate:

why they exist (purpose),

what they will do (goals and actions), and

how this will be accomplished (practices).

Missions start with "the end in mind" and become a map that can be used to guide actions and help you stay on course.

Review the class mission statement on the next page.

Locate the mission statement of your school; review and discuss.

Locate and discuss the mission statements of two businesses or companies.

Use an affinity diagram to create a mission statement for this class.

Ask and answer:

Why are we here?

What do we need to do well together?

How will we make this happen?

What do you want to learn in this class?

Write a draft of your class mission statement.

V. Complete Your Class Mission Statement

Review the mission statement below.
1. *Note important words or phrases.*
2. *Can you identify the "what, why, and how" in this mission statement?*
3. *In your opinion, is the illustration important? Explain your answer.*
4. *Review the core values students stated they will use to accomplish their mission. Core values are things we believe are important and use to guide how we work and interact with others. Respect and leadership are core values.*
5. *Review values you identified in the the Introduction.*
6. *Revisit and discuss: www.values.com/pass-it-on-downloads Relate to your mission statement.*
7. *Complete an affinity diagram to determine values important to you and your class to work well together and accomplish goals.*

> "We, the students of the second-hour Life Skills class at Rocinante High School, have chosen to complete our educations and graduate. We will identify, increase, and use options and resources in a caring learning environment of choice.
>
> We will accomplish this by:
> - supporting and respecting each other
> - taking leadership roles
> - attending class on time and prepared
> - striving to keep campus safe."

Review your draft mission statement.
Write your class mission statement here.

VI. Rubrics

Rubrics are used to clarify expectations and identify levels of achievement. The rubric at the end of each chapter in *The R Rules* is used to assess learning and to plan. Use this rubric to define and clarify the values and behaviors you listed in your classroom mission statement.

	4	3	2	1
Respect				

Follow these steps to create a rubric:

Step 1: Identify 3–5 items that will be evaluated.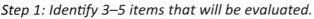
   (Rocinante students listed respect, being prepared, leadership, and keeping campus safe.)
Step 2: Set up a grid with numerical values (generally 1–4).
Step 3: Identify characteristics that are excellent or exceeding standards.
   List those in the column marked 4. (Begin with the end in mind.)
Step 4: Work backwards. Identify characteristics for 3, 2, and 1 and list in each column.
Step 5: Evaluate using the criteria listed for each item under each number.

Create a Rubric for Your Class

Review your class mission statement. Identify core values and behaviors.
Break into teams. Each team will develop the rubric for one core value.
Teams present rubrics to class. Revise as needed.
Class agrees and accepts the rubric.
Post rubric in classroom and file a copy in personal planners.
Review rubric regularly and make revisions as needed.

VII. SMART Goals and Action Plans: Write SMART Goals

SMART GOALS

The parts of a goal are:
who, what, when, how.

SMART goals are:
Specific, can be **Measured**, and have an **Action, Results,** and a **Timeline.**

Specific	Measurement	Actions	Results	Timeline
WHO will do WHAT, WHEN, to reach the goal or desired outcome, and HOW success will be measured.	**WHAT** What is the focus of the goal? What will be done or accomplished? What measurement will be used to determine success?	**HOW** How will improvement be measured? How will achieving the goal be determined?	**HOW** The outcome or measure of what was achieved. Realistic Relevant Resources	**WHEN** When work on the goal will start; the target date to accomplish the goal; the deadline, or when the work will stop.

S → Specific
M → Measurable
A → Action
R → Results
T → Timeline

Steps for writing a SMART goal:

1. Begin with the end in mind. Ask: What do I want to do? Why? Check the cards in your hand and your future picture.
2. Write a *SMART* goal. Be *Specific*. Include *Measures, Action, Results,* and *Timeline*.
   a. Determine who—you, a group, a class—is writing the goal.
   b. Analyze information and data to decide *what* your goal will be.
   c. Decide *what* you will work on—what you will accomplish or improve.
   d. Decide *when* you will start working on the goal and when work will end (time, dates).
   e. Choose *how* you will measure results and success. How will you know you met your goal?
   f. Keep goals in your personal planner.
3. Write and use an action plan to manage, monitor progress, and make revisions.

Start Date: _____ Target Date or Stop Date: _____

_____ will _____

by _____ as measured by _____.

I will know my goal has been reached _____.

I will check progress toward this goal on _____.

Chapter 1—Road Trip

VII. TRANSLATING Your Ideas into SMART Goals and Actions

How could these statements be written into SMART goals? "Get better grades." "Win." "Get in shape." "Get my driver's license." "Improve my communication skills." "More time."

 Is this a SMART goal and action plan?

I will increase my grade in English from a C to a B by October 15.

To do this I will:
Complete and turn in all assignments,
attend after-school tutoring, and
check my grades once a week.

I will know my goal has been achieved when the
English grade on my October 20 report card is a B.

I will begin working on October 1. Work will end on October 15.
I will meet with Ms. Jones to check progress on October 6, 11, and 14.

S _____

M _____

A _____

R _____

T _____

Use a note card.
Fold into five sections.
Write one letter on each section: S-M-A-R-T.
Write your goal and accomplish it!

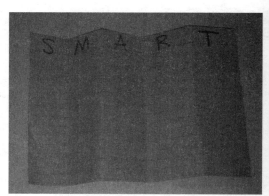

–Kate Mikle, Menominee Indian School District

VII. TRANSLATING Your SMART Goals into Actions and Plans

Use these forms to chunk out steps to reach a goal.
One goal may have several strategies.
Write a separate set of action steps for each strategy.

Goal:				
Strategy:				
Action Steps	Who Is Responsible	Timeline	Resources	Completion Measure

Goal				
Strategy	Action Steps	Who Is Responsible	Timeline	How Measured
1.				
2.				
3.				
4.				

VII. TRANSLATING Your Goals into Actions

1. ASK and ANSWER: WHAT, WHY, HOW
  A.
      1. What   2. Why   3. How
        Wash the car
  B.
      1. What   2. Why   3. How
        Buy a car

2. CREATE and USE LISTS and STEP SHEETS
Checklists and to-do lists are great tools to manage jobs and accomplish tasks. Brainstorm and list everything you need to do. Check off or draw a line through each item as it is completed.
LIST IN:
A. *Random order:* Brainstorm what you need to do and list it **in any order.**
B. *Logical order:* Brainstorm what you need to do.
        List actions or steps **in the order in which they need to be and will be done.**
C. *Order of priority:* Brainstorm what you need to do, list, organize **in order of importance.**
        List and do most important first, least important last.

To-Do Lists		
A. Random	**B.** Logical—Step by Step	**C.** Priority
	1	1
	2	2
	3	3
	4	4
		5

3. FUTURE PICTURE
Check day-to-day activities to determine if they are helping you move toward your future picture or if they are just keeping you busy. Coach John Wooden, who led 10 UCLA basketball teams to NCAA championships, said that one of his "secrets of success" is to "never mistake activity for achievement."

Goal Mobile

VIII. Planning Backwards

Monday	Tuesday	Wednesday	Thursday	Friday	Saturday	Sunday
1. 2. 3. 4. 5.	1. 2. 3. 4. 5.	1. 2. 3. 4. 5.	1. 2. 3. 4. 5.	1. 2. 3. 4. 5.	1. 2. 3. 4. 5.	1. 2. 3. 4. 5.

VIII. Planning Backwards

To Plan, Organize, and Manage Time
Begin with the End in Mind

4 _____

4 _____

4 _____

VIII. Plan Backwards
To Plan, Organize, and Manage Begin with the End in Mind

Sunday	Monday	Tuesday	Wednesday	Thursday	Friday	Saturday

See additional planning backwards forms on pp. 246–249.

IX. TEAMWORK
Build a Community of Learners and Leaders

1. Complete the teamwork activity.

2. As a class, use a force field diagram to identify drivers and barriers related to working as a team.

3. Discuss, identify resources, and work together to clarify and agree on behaviors you will use.

⟶   ⟵

Schedule Game Days!
Schedule game days and use them to develop teamwork and interpersonal skills and have fun.
Discuss rules, procedures, and policies.
Invite community members to your classroom to teach and learn new games.
Organize a tournament, compete against other classes, or develop as a service project.

X. Project Management
Organize, Manage, and Complete a Project

Project development and management are skills needed to succeed at school, work, and in life. Listed here are steps to identify, develop, manage, and complete a project. Each step will take time, and the project may continue for the entire school year. Work as a class, guided by your instructor, using procedures and resources to complete a project or projects that will make a difference in your school and/or community.

1. Brainstorm ideas to make a positive difference in your community or school.
2. Use an affinity diagram to gather ideas and identify possible projects.
3. Vote to narrow down the number of projects you will consider.
4. Assign a team to investigate and research each project.
5. Work as teams to research each of the projects. Report to class on:
    a. What the project will accomplish and why there is a need
    b. What resources will be needed: transportation, money, time, materials, approval, etc.
    c. Other organizations or clubs that have similar projects that you might partner with
    d. Short- and long-term activities, benefits, and outcomes
    e. Action steps, processes, and timelines
    f. How you will measure the success of the project
6. As a class, determine and agree on the project or projects that will be worked on.
7. Build teams.
    a. State the goal for each project—what will be done or accomplished
    b. Identify teams and roles—manager, time keeper, recorder, reporter, etc.
    c. Assign tasks based on interests, strengths, and resources
    d. Discuss processes, procedures, and policies
    e. Clarify standards and expectations—may use a rubric
8. Develop action plans and use them to organize, manage, and complete projects.
    a. Review the goal
    b. Brainstorm actions to reach the goal
    c. Organize the actions in the order they will be done
    d. Write start dates and end dates for each action
    e. Determine who will do what, when, and how
    f. How you will know the action is completed
9. Develop a process to report on activities, progress, and challenges.
10. Review and use the project log on the following page to keep track of your work.
11. Make a difference and have fun!

Project planning ideas at:
http://www.p21.org/storage/documents/Skills%20Map/Project_Management_Skills_Map_Final.pdf

	PROJECT	Hours
	Total Hours	

X. Organize, Manage, and Complete a Project
Combine Tools

Chunk it. Identify resources. Prioritize. Determine "time to task." Plan backwards.

1. What needs to be done?	Why? – the goal	2. How? – resources
Have a party		
Present to the school board		

3. What will you do first?
1.
2.
3.
4.
5.
6.
7.
8.

4. How much time will this take?
1.
2.
3.
4.
5.
6.
7.
8.

1:00	2:00	3:00	4:00	5:00	6:00
					5.

1. Brainstorm and make a list of what will be done and why.
2. List resources you will need. If you are missing a resource, add getting it to your list of tasks.
3. List tasks in the order you will do them.
4. Determine how much time each activity will take.
5. Use the amount of time you have for the project and plan backwards to schedule.
6. Implement your plan and adjust as needed to complete your work.
7. Use what you learn to plan and schedule future activities and projects.

XI. R Rules Raffiti

Recall ideas, quotes, or words that inspired you while exploring values.com and writing a mission statement.

List words or values you live by:

Life is like a journey.
If you were a car, what would you look like?

When you come to a
fork in the road—
take the right one.

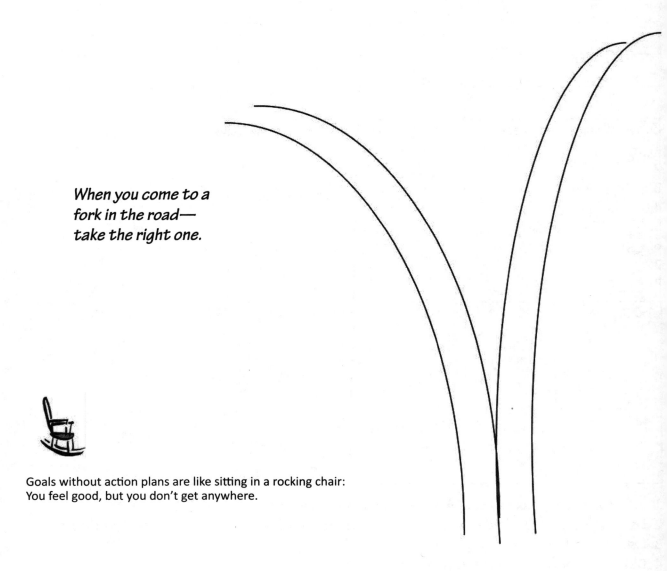

Goals without action plans are like sitting in a rocking chair:
You feel good, but you don't get anywhere.

XI. Rubric for Road Trip

1. Begin with the End in Mind
2. Time Maps
3. Tools—Manage and Patterns
4. Mission Statement
5. Rubrics and Class Rubric
6. SMART Goals and Action Plans
7. Planning Backwards
8. Teamwork
9. Project Development and Management
10. Raffiti, Reflect, Reference

4.0	I understand the chapter and can teach the concepts I learned to others. What I learned is important and can be used in the following ways:
3.0	I understand the chapter and do not have any questions about the concepts. What I learned is important because:
2.0	I understand parts of this chapter. I still don't understand and have questions about:
1.0	I still need help to understand the basic concepts of this chapter. Specifically about:

My plan to use what I learned in this chapter:

Rubric by K. Dixon

XI. Road Trip Definitions, Symbols, Mental Models, Tools

Definitions

Action plan: Steps to accomplish a goal.

Action steps: Actions steps to accomplish the goal or strategy.

Advocate: Person or group who supports or argues for a cause or policy. Someone who supports or promotes the interests of another.

Goal: What will be accomplished or completed: "the end in mind."

Momentum and milestone years: Momentum years are a mental model for times when you were traveling or moving toward your goal or future picture. Milestone years are a mental model for the place or time you met your goal. Actual milestones are the series of numbered markers placed at intervals of one mile on roads and highways.

Procedure: Formal instructions that are followed and state how something will be done.

Project: A collaborative effort involving research, planning, and actions to achieve a specific outcome.

Strategy: The plan or actions that will be used to accomplish a goal.

Timeline: A schedule of events in the order they will occur. Action plans include start dates, completion or stop dates, and dates to check progress.

Tradition: Beliefs or behaviors passed down or honored within a group that have special meaning or significance in relation to the past.

Symbols and Mental Models

 R Rules mental model for discussion; recycling ideas and information

XI. Road Trip Definitions, Symbols, Mental Models, Tools

Tool

Affinity Diagram

Tool to gather and sort ideas and classify, categorize, organize, and group information.

Step 1: Write or state the topic or question.
Step 2: Brainstorm ideas related to the topic or issue (silently or talk out).
Step 3: Each participant writes their ideas or responses on sticky notes.
     Use a different sticky note for each response. One response per sticky.
Step 4: Participants post their sticky notes in random order in designated area.
Step 5: Sort the sticky notes into groups that are similar, related, or connected.
Step 6: For each group, select a title to describe the category or classification.

Topic: _____

Title or Category	Category	Category	Category
Idea			
Idea			
Idea			
Idea			
Idea			
Idea			

Chapter 2 Relevance—Learning Objectives

I. What Is Relevant to You?	Understanding relevance is a 21st century skill.	Use scenarios and examples to investigate relevance.
II. Situational Awareness	Necessary to navigate and achieve in situations, systems, and environments at work, school, and in life.	Increase awareness of patterns relevant to achievement in various situations and environments.
III. Your Future Picture	Planners and future pictures are used to guide conferences, check progress, and gather and use feedback.	Conference using R Rules Personal Planner. Assess personal progress, learning styles, and use patterns to build resources.
IV. Ask What, Why, How	Tools to identify and sort what is important from what is not important.	Ask what, why, how: to sort for importance and response; to summarize; to take notes.
V. Root Cause Five Whys	Process to identify root cause, problem solving, response, and workplace skills and readiness.	Problem solve, think critically, and respond.
VI. Cause and Effect If-Then	Understand the relevance of cause and effect and predicting in order to plan and respond.	Use processes to identify relevant factors, be in control, problem solve, predict, and plan.
VII. Patterns	If you can identify a pattern, you can predict. If you can predict, you can plan.	Understand and apply patterns to plan, predict, organize, manage, and reach goals.
VIII. The Relevance of Voice	Understand the relevance of voice to achievement, relationships, and building personal resources.	Develop voice to negotiate and communicate. Use procedural and positive self-talk to guide and inspire.
IX. Check It!	Check for understanding and application.	Give examples and discuss information in this chapter.
X. Relevance of Resources	Understanding of resources relevant to reaching a future picture and achieving.	Read a scenario and discuss the relevance of resources to reaching a future picture.
XI. Raffiti, Rubric, Definitions	Clarify information, define mental models, and reflect.	Build knowledge, resources, and vocabulary.
Check items to be filed in your R Rules Personal Planner.		

Chapter 2—Relevance

Knowing when or why something is important.

Understanding the connection or relationship to the outcome.

I. R^u What Is Relevant to You?

What is relevant to wearing sunglasses?
How relevant are your friends to the choices you make?
What values and characteristics are relevant when choosing a friend?
What is relevant to a successful job interview?
What factors are relevant to the job or career in your future picture?
What is relevant to success?
How are relationships relevant to learning?

II. Situational Awareness

Another aspect of "relevance" is situational awareness—being aware of what is relevant or important in a situation or environment. Situational awareness is the ability to see different factors and patterns in environments relative to yourself and goals. It basically means knowing what is going on around you.

The U.S. Coast Guard defines situational awareness as "the ability to identify, to process, and to comprehend critical elements of information about what is happening with regards to the mission." The key to using situational awareness is the ability to—like the Coast Guard—connect the information to your mission or an outcome. Great athletes develop keen situational awareness. They read the patterns of teams and individual players, determine what is relevant in changing situations, and use that information to predict, play, and win. Businesses, schools, and groups all have "distinct" patterns and habits that have developed over time, are relevant to achievement, and become accepted behaviors of the group.

Develop situational awareness to identify and understand what is relevant to success in various systems and environments. Use the information to help reach your future picture. If you don't have a situational awareness card in your hand, consider adding one.

Listen to the facilitator read the story, "A Million Ideas."
Discuss and reflect on the relevance of situational awareness.

II. Situational Awareness

What is relevant in any situation?
Location is relevant. Environments are relevant. Experiences are relevant. Language is relevant. People are relevant. We all have and use different mental models about how the world is and should be. Mental models are relevant—they are related to our personal experiences and knowledge. They are the cards we use to play the game. Sometimes other players have the same cards; sometimes the cards are different.

Take this little quiz ...

1. If something occurs *most of the time,* it occurs _____% of the time.

2. If you tell someone on the phone, "I'll do that *right away,*" how long will it be before you start working on it?

3. If you tell someone you are busy, but you also say, "I will get to it *as soon as possible,*" how long will "as soon as possible" be?

4. If you are invited to dinner at a friend's house, what time will you arrive?

5. A friend introduces you to his or her grandpa. What does the term "grandpa" mean or tell you?

6. You wore your best clothes to a job interview. What did you wear?

7. Draw a giraffopotamus.

We are all different.
We are all alike.

Quiz adapted from the work of Janet Peregoy.

III. Your Future Picture

In this chapter you will use tools, processes, and patterns to explore and determine what is relevant to you.

Use your personal planner, investigate your learning and leadership styles, and identify your individual strengths and talents.

Use your future picture—what you want to be, do, and have—to determine what is relevant and important to you. Use that information to help when making choices, decisions, and when responding. If you don't know what you want to do or be, switch the pattern and consider what you don't want to do or be, then "plan backwards."

1. Complete a personal planner review
Follow process for conference and planner review.
Winners are determined by an event. Champions require a process.

2. Assess learning styles
Go to http://www.edutopia.org/multiple-intelligences-learning-styles-quiz
Complete the learning style inventory; print and review results.
File a copy in your planner. Explore the site; take notes on learning styles, multiple intelligences, and other information related to learning that you find of interest.

Go to http://www.educationplanner.org/students/self-assessments/learning-styles-quiz.shtml and complete the learning style inventory and character strength quiz.
Explore the site, take notes, and assess how you will use the information.
File a copy in your planner.
Discussion: What is the relevance of the three letters at the end of a website?
What are the differences between websites ending in .edu, .org, or .com?

✋ A little brain research
From Dr. G. Phillips, National School Improvement Project

We learn and remember after one month ...
14% of what we hear
22% of what we see
30% of what we watch others do: demonstrations
42% sensory redundancy: classroom rituals
72% movies of the mind: remembered images
83% performance of a life challenge activity
92% of the information is retained when we teach others

 How can you use this information?

Name

	0	.5	1	1.5	2	2.5	3	3.5	4											

R^U Progress Check developed by K. Dixon and B. Souther.

IV. Ask What, Why, and How Tools to Sort for Relevance

1. To Sort for Importance

What	WHY	How

2. To Summarize or Take Notes

How	Why	WHAT

https://www.youtube.com/watch?v=WtW9IyE04OQ

3. To Sort for Response

What	Why	HOW
		🕐

V. Root Cause

There was a problem with the Jefferson Memorial located in Washington, DC. The granite was crumbling, and the memorial was going to be lost. Park officials were frustrated because none of the other memorials were having a similar problem. There were many theories about why the granite was crumbling. To solve the problem and get to the "root cause," ask and answer "Why?"

1. *Why* is the granite crumbling on the Jefferson Memorial?
   Answer: It is washed off more than the other memorials.
2. *Why* is the Jefferson Memorial washed off more than the other DC memorials?
   Answer: The Jefferson Memorial has more bird dung.
3. *Why* does the Jefferson Memorial have more bird dung than other DC memorials?
   Answer: It has more birds.
4. *Why* does the Jefferson Memorial have more birds?
   Answer: It has more spiders for the birds to eat.
5. *Why* does the Jefferson Memorial have more spiders?
   Answer: It has more flying insects for the spiders to eat.
6. *Why* does the Jefferson Memorial have more flying insects than other DC memorials?
   Answer: The lights are turned on first and off last at the Jefferson Memorial. The lights are on longer at the Jefferson Memorial, which attracts more insects.

Solution: The schedule was changed, and the lights were turned on later at the Jefferson Memorial. The crumbling stopped. Ask why at least five times to get to the root or root cause of a problem.

https://www.youtube.com/watch?v=IETtnK7gzlE
https://www.youtube.com/watch?v=qiUPHbFzA4M

Root Cause = Try Five Whys

Step 1. State the current situation or problem.
Step 2. Restate the problem or situation in the form of a question. Why ...
Step 3. Answer this question.
Step 4. Based on the answer to this question, ask another question. Why ...
Step 5. Continue this pattern for five questions or until the root cause is determined.
Step 6. Develop an action plan.

VI. Relevance of Cause and Effect

If-then is a tool to identify patterns of cause and effect.
1. In the IF box write the topic, situation, or event (cause).
2. In the THEN box write what occurred (effect).
OR
2. In the THEN box write how you will respond or the next step (effect).
OR
2. In the THEN box write what you predict will occur or a new prediction (effect).
3. Complete this process five times or until you reach a solution.

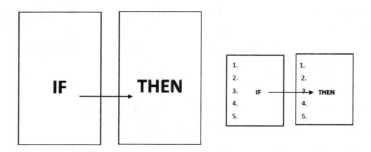

A tool to identify relevance, cause and effect, and plan and predict.

Step 1: In the IF box, write the current situation, topic, or prediction.
Step 2: In the THEN box, write what happened, the next step, or a new prediction.
Step 3: Repeat for five rounds or until the end of the story or problem.

If-then is a process used to identify relevant factors, options, predict, and plan.

If she says ⟶ then I'll say

If we are going to have a party ⟶ then

If my car won't start ⟶ then

If the baby keeps crying ⟶ then

If the trees are not growing ⟶ then

If I plan to graduate this spring ⟶ then

If you could help me understand ⟶ then

If my future picture is ⟶ then

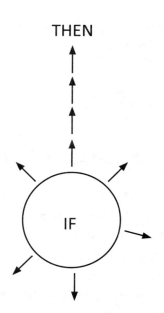

Source: J. Pfarr Consulting

VI. Relevance of Cause and Effect

1. Work in teams of two.
2. Use the form below to show the if-then process. Use one of the statements on the previous page or create your own.
3. Write the "if" statement in Square 1, and apply the if-then process five times.
    Example: 1. "If you are missing a grade for an assignment you know you turned in … "
         1. "Then … "

1. If	1. Then
2. If	2. Then
3. If	3. Then
4. If	4. Then
5. If	5. Then

4. Use the circle model (previous page) to show multiple responses to the same "if" statement.

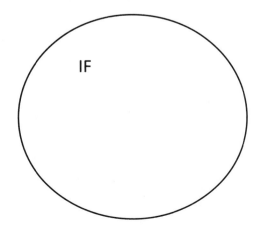

Chapter 2—Relevance

VII. Patterns

*If you can see a pattern—
you can predict.
If you can predict—
you can plan.
If you can plan—
you can …*

Patterns are the way the mind sorts information. Patterns are consistently recurring events, characteristics, behaviors, or features. When you look in the mirror, your mind is organizing approximately 29,000 pieces of information into a pattern that it uses to sort, identify, and recognize your face. And all of this takes place in less than a nanosecond and without any conscious effort on your part!

Situational awareness requires identifying and understanding the relevance of patterns. Patterns can be observed in any environment or process. Habits are patterns. There are patterns at school. Procedures and processes follow a pattern. Mathematical processes—such as addition or subtraction—follow a pattern. There are patterns in nature. Seasons follow an order or pattern. Geese fly in a "V" formation for safety and efficiency.

The ability to identify and follow patterns—consciously or unconsciously—can save time, energy, and reduce stress. Develop your ability to see patterns, understand their relevance, and use them in different situations, environments, and systems. Use information to check personal habits, plan, and predict in order to behave and respond in ways that will get the results and respect you want.

Present an example, and discuss the relevance of a pattern
An example would be a book. Books follow a pattern. They have a title page, table of contents, chapters, paragraphs, numbered pages, and they use bold print for important topics. Information can be located faster if you know and follow the pattern. Possible topics to show the relevance of a pattern: sports, music, genres, colleges, nature, a building, a job, a personal routine, technology, fashion, time, people, cultures, customs, marketing, or a topic of your choice.

VII. Patterns

Demonstrate one of the six organizational patterns below using an illustration, example, story, diagram, graphic organizer, or activity.

Organizational patterns
1. Chronological patterns are organized according to time.
2. Sequential patterns are organized by related events or actions that follow each other.
3. Cause and effect patterns show the effects—results of the cause—reasons.
4. Compare and contrast patterns identify how two or more things are similar or different.
5. Classification patterns organize elements into groups based on their similarities.
6. Alphabetical patterns organize elements in the order of the alphabet.

VIII. The Relevance of Voice

Patterns of:
Body language
Facial expression
Tone
Voice …

We all get three voices—a child voice, a parent voice, and an adult voice. Each voice has a distinct pattern.

Child voice is the voice of a victim. It is defensive and blames others. It is full of emotion—angry, fearful, whiny, helpless, from a position of losing. Child voice can also be playful, curious, teasing, manipulative, or can diffuse anger. Body language is negative and/or exaggerated.

Dependent

Quit picking on me.
You don't love me.
You make me mad.
He said. She said.
That's not fair!
It's not my fault!

Don't blame me. It's not my fault!
Nobody likes/loves me.
So, what was I supposed to do?
I never get to. She always gets to!
I had to.
I couldn't help it.

VIII. The Relevance of Voice

We all get three voices—a child voice, a parent voice, and an adult voice. Each voice has a distinct pattern.

Parent voice is one of authority. It directs, comes from a position of power.
Can be both positive and negative.
Directs, is voice of authority.
Is used to take charge of or stop a situation.
Questions, gives orders, comes from a place of authority and power.
Can be threatening, demanding, judgmental, and criticize.

Can show concern and be supportive, but can also cause shame or guilt.
Body language can be controlling, angry, impatient, pointing finger, loud voice.

Independent

Don't do that!
Where are you going?
You are just lazy!
STOP THAT!
You do as I say.
You are wrong.

What is wrong with you?
What did you think would happen?
If you were more like your brother ...
Are you all right?
Quit worrying about it.
Leave the room right now.

Adult voice is the voice of negotiation.
This voice best supports learning, resolving conflict, and building relationships.
It is factual, seeks to understand.
Is nonjudgmental, can listen and learn, respects.
Invites parties in conversation to talk about an idea or situation.
It is the voice of win-win.
Body language is nonthreatening, often leaning forward, attentive, respectful.

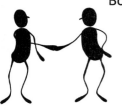

Interdependent

What would you like to see ... ?
Can we work together to ... ?
We agree to disagree.
What are our choices?
What is your plan?

Can you help me understand ... ?
How do you see this resolved?
What could we do to improve this?
How can ... ?
Would you consider ... ?

Three voices from the work of Eric Berne and Ruby Payne.

VIII. The Relevance of Voice

Key Points

1. The adult voice is directed at the outcome or situation—not the person.
2. Begin a conversation in (or change to) the voice you want the conversation to end in.
3. To teach, learn, and build relationships, use the adult voice.
4. The child voice will stall conversations.
5. The child voice can defuse anger when used in a teasing or playful manner.
6. To control or stop a situation, use the parent voice.
   Follow the parent voice with the adult voice to redirect and provide a strategy.
   For example, "Stop!" "Get out of the street." "You could get hurt."
   "Next time, take my hand and we can cross together."
7. Voice includes body language and nonverbals.
8. We all have three voices in our heads and can use them to talk to ourselves—this is called "self-talk."
9. Self-talk in the parent voice can be used to stop behaviors.
10. Self-talk in the parent voice can be judgmental or critical and cause fear, guilt, or shame.
11. Positive self-talk motivates, encourages, honors, and affirms.
12. Procedural self-talk is the voice used to organize, work through a situation or process, and follow steps to complete a project.

IX. Check It!

1. How can understanding self-talk help you reach your future picture? Give an example of positive and procedural self-talk.

2. How can understanding voices help you reach your future picture? Give an example of language to negotiate.

Working in teams of three:
3. Each person draws one card. Cards are labeled: child, parent, or adult. Each person uses the voice on the card they drew to carry on a conversation about the school cafeteria.

4. Answer the question: Which voice does a bully use? Report out to the class and discuss. Justify your answer.

5. Discuss the data below relative to school, a job, and a personal relationship.

Communication is:
7% words
38% tone and emotion
53% body language

Which cards will you add to your hand?

Which cards will you discard?

IX. Check It!

Make a mark for each time you hear one of these voices.
Review your results. Look for patterns. Discuss.
Do you use all three voices?

	Child	Parent	Adult
7:00 to 10:00			
10:00 to 12:00			
12:00 to 2:00			
2:00 to 4:00			
4:00 to 7:00			
7:00 to 10:00			
10:00 to 12:00			

Which voice does the person you are dating use most often?

Which voice do you use most often?

IX. Check It!

Karpman Triangle (Drama Triangle): Victim, Bully, Rescuer
The Empowerment Dynamic (TED): Champion, Challenger, Coach

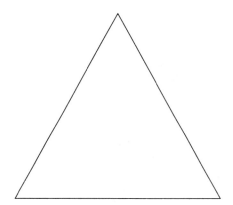
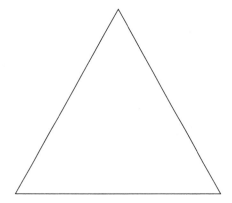

X. Relevance of Resources

David

In *The R Rules* resources are defined as anything available to a person, institution, or community that can be used to assist, support, or help. Resources are relevant because success is often determined by the resources that are available, or the lack of them. Consider David's resources as you read the story. We all have resources, and like David we all start with the cards we were dealt.

David was a thin young man with dark eyes and a presence beyond his 17 years. All through my training he sat quietly, listening and taking notes. As I finished my presentation and was preparing to leave, David walked over and asked me a question.

David was a Grade Court student. Grade Court is a program in my community that offers juvenile offenders the option of trading cell time for time in the classroom to earn credits and diplomas. Certified teachers provide instruction and monitor the progress of the participants, who report to the court on a regular basis. Our college worked with Grade Court, and I had just provided a one-day session on goal setting and management skills. Later that month, the class was scheduled to take a tour of the college.

David asked me if I worked at the college. I explained my connection and asked him how I might help. He told me that he was close to completing his Grade Court hours and was preparing for the GED (General Educational Development) test. As part of the program, when he received his GED the college would give him a scholarship. The problem was that he didn't know how to register for classes. A call to the college set up a meeting at the college for David. On the day of the scheduled tour, someone from admissions would meet David and help him through the maze of registration.

On Friday the bus came to the school, and all of the students, anxious and ready for the trip, quickly boarded—all of the students except one. David was not there. We waited on this hot summer day with no air conditioning on the bus, and the temperature rising—my hope dropping. We waited five minutes. Then ten. All the kids knew how important this was to David, and each time I wanted to leave, they kept insisting we wait. As an old blue car chugged into the parking lot, there was a collective sigh of relief. David—black hair glistening and tied back, dressed in a new, navy blue T-shirt, gold chain, Levis with a crease, tennis shoes scrubbed clean—smiled and boarded the bus.

David met with the director of admissions at the college that day. He enrolled and has been taking classes for the past two years, working to earn an associate's degree. He is going to be a graphic designer.

X. Relevance of Resources

David

I learned later how hard David worked to make it to the college tour that day. Between the time I met David and the day we took the tour, David's mother had a medical crisis. David had driven her the 35 miles to and from the hospital where she qualifies to receive free medical services.

David completed his Grade Court hours and passed his GED exam. He also worked extra hours at his part-time job because his baby was sick. Medicaid paid the hospital fees; David had to find money for the prescriptions.

One resource can be the difference between success or failure, hitting or missing your goal. How resources are used is as relevant to success as the amount or type of the resources. Each of us has resources. For David, one small resource—a relationship that could provide the information and access to register for college—was all he needed.

Resources are relevant and interrelated. Each resource influences the others. Understanding patterns, resources, and relationships will help you see connections, predict, and make plans to achieve your future picture.

Life is like a card game.
You can't control the cards you are dealt.
You can control how you play them.

XI. R Rules Raffiti

A pattern:
    Two ears—one mouth.
    Listen twice—talk once.

What is relevant to you?

We are all alike.
    We are all different.

"Men and women are not only themselves;
they are also the region in which they were born,
the city apartment or the farm in which they learnt to walk,
the games they played as children, the old wives' tales they overheard,
the food they ate, the schools they attended, the sports they followed,
the poets they read, and the God they believed in."
—W. Somerset Maugham

XI. Relevance

1. Situational Awareness
2. Future Picture and Planner Review
3. What, Why, How
4. Root Cause—Five Whys
5. Cause and Effect—If-Then
6. Patterns
7. Voice
8. Resources
9. Raffiti, Reflect, Reference

4.0	I understand the chapter and can teach the concepts I learned to others. What I learned is important and can be used in the following ways:
3.0	I understand the chapter and do not have any questions about the concepts. What I learned is important because:
2.0	I understand parts of this chapter. I still don't understand and have questions about:
1.0	I still need help to understand the basic concepts of this chapter. Specifically about:

How I will use what I learned in this chapter:

Rubric by K. Dixon

XI. Relevance Definitions, Symbols, Mental Models, Tools

Definitions

Body language: Nonverbal movements and mannerisms a person uses to communicate with others. Examples: posture, gestures, facial expressions. May or may not be intentional.

Genre: A classification or category of literature or other form of art or entertainment, such as music, that is based on a particular form, content, or technique. Can be in written, spoken, audio, or visual format.

Illustrate: To explain or make something clear by using examples, charts, pictures, etc.

Learning styles: Different styles and techniques individuals use to collect, organize, and turn information into useful knowledge or learning.

Multiple intelligences: Dr. Howard Gardner's theory that people are smart in different ways.

Situational awareness: Ability to identify factors and patterns in different environments. It is basically knowing what is going on around you.

Symbols and Mental Models

 R Rules mental model for discussion, recycling ideas, and information

 R Rules mental model for hope and resources

Chapter 3 Resources—Learning Objectives

What?	Why?	How?
I. Key Points	Present key information about resources.	Review to check for prior knowledge and understanding.
II. Resources	Resources help, assist, and support. Resources are relevant to achievement at work, at school, and in life.	Understand 10 basic resources using a hand as a mental model. Identify and develop personal resources.
III. Resource Check	Use case studies to identify and understand resources.	Review David's and Larissa's stories and scenarios to identify and build resources.
IV. Check Your Cards	Rate personal resources—high, medium, low—in order to plan.	Apply information relevant to current and future pictures.
V. Current and Future Pictures	Use mental model of current and future picture to plan and achieve future picture.	Use mental models to plan, identify action steps, and build resources.
VI. A Little Quiz	Discussion and assessment of resources and hidden rules.	Respond to questions, discuss, and journal about resources.
VII. Community Resource Project	Increase awareness, access and develop community resources, and contribute to community.	Identify, develop, publish, and distribute listing of resources available to community.
VIII. Social Capital	Social capital is a resource; it builds networks and options for individuals and communities.	Identify and increase personal and community social capital.
IX. 21st Century Skills	This website explains and identifies skills relevant to success in the 21st century.	Explore website to increase understanding and personal benefit. Present information to classmates.
X. Plus Delta Evaluation	Tool to provide feedback and increase communication and leadership skills.	Develop skills as an evaluator and presenter.
XI. Resources	Resources are unique to systems and individuals.	Use mental model to see how resources vary depending on the individual and situation.
XII. Raffiti, Rubric, Definitions	Clarify information and reflect; define mental models and tools.	Build knowledge, resources, and vocabulary.
Check items to be filed in your R Rules Personal Planner.		

Chapter 3—Resources

Resources—Anything available to an individual, institution, or community that can be used to assist, support, or help.

Work in teams.
Review the definition above.
 Timekeeper – 15 minutes
Identify and list examples of resources: school, home, work, in your community.
Report out.

I. Key Points

1. We all have resources. We all get a set of cards.
2. Resources are anything that can be used to assist, support, or help.
3. We use the resources that are available to meet challenges and live well.
4. This chapter will present 10 resources.
5. Resources are connected, interrelated, and are used in relationship to other resources.
6. Resources can be internal (self-control); resources can be external (a friend).
7. Resources are relevant to situations, systems, and environments.
8. *The R Rules* defines under-resourced as not having the resources to address a particular situation or navigate a particular environment.
9. Poverty is defined as the extent to which an individual, institution, or community does without resources.
10. Resources = choices. More resources = more choices.
11. Use *The R Rules* to identify, develop, and access personal and community resources.

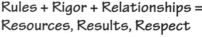

**Rules + Rigor + Relationships =
Resources, Results, Respect**

II. Resources

1. **Financial**
   Having money to purchase goods and services.

2. **Physical**
   Having physical health and mobility that allows you to be self-sufficient in order to learn, earn, and lead.

3. **Emotional**
   The ability to choose and control emotional responses, particularly in negative situations, without engaging in self-destructive behavior. This is an internal resource and shows itself through stability, stamina, perseverance, and choices.

4. **Mental**
   Having the mental abilities and acquired skills (reading, writing, and computing) to manage and deal with daily life.

5. **Spiritual**
   Believing in a purpose, a power greater than yourself, divine guidance, and a future picture. Hope. A source of personal strength and motivation.

6. **Support Systems**
   Having backup resources, supports, friends, and family available and willing to listen and assist when needed. Who can you count on that will not ask you to engage in destructive behavior? These are external resources.

7. **Relationships**
   Having frequent access to individuals in relationships of *mutual* respect who are appropriate, who care, and who do not engage in self-destructive behaviors or ask you to engage in them either.

8. **Role Models**
   Having individuals who serve as models to guide personal choices, actions, and behaviors. May be an individual you know or someone you have only observed or read about. Two types of role models: positive and negative.

9. **Knowledge of Hidden Rules**
   Knowing the unspoken cues and habits of a group. Having situational awareness; understanding rules and resources to navigate and achieve in different systems, situations, and environments.

10. **Language**
    Having the ability to use formal register; communicate, collaborate, and negotiate in a variety of forms and contexts—at school, at work, and in life.

II. Resources

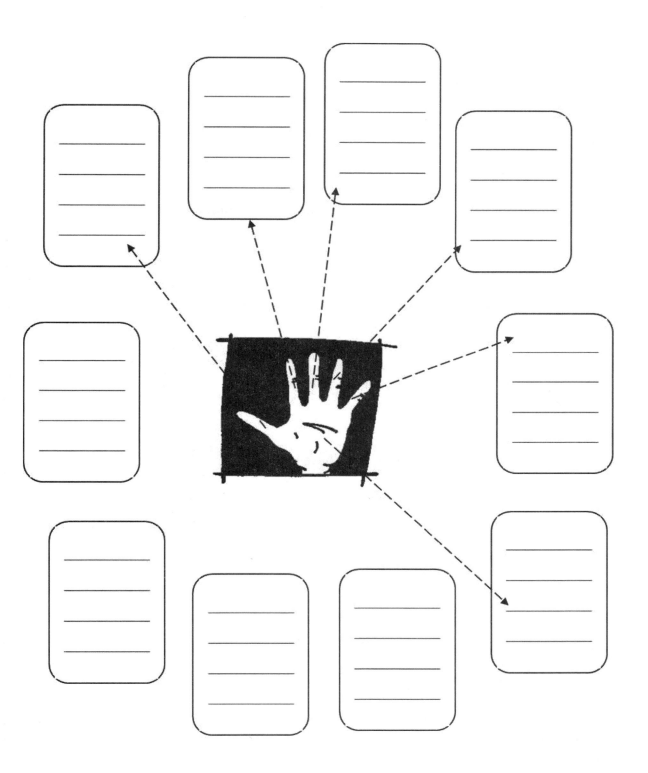

92% of information is retained when it is learned in order to teach to others.

III. Resource Check

Review David's story on page 68 in Chapter 2.
Which of the resources below did David have?

Financial	Mental	Relationships
Physical	Spiritual	Role Models
Emotional	Support Systems	Hidden Rules
Language		

Review Larissa's story on page 13 in the Introduction.
Which of these resources did Larissa have?

Financial	Mental	Relationships
Physical	Spiritual	Role Models
Emotional	Support Systems	Hidden Rules
Language		

Review your story. Which of these resources do you have?

Financial	Mental	Relationships
Physical	Spiritual	Role Models
Emotional	Support Systems	Hidden Rules
Language		

How are David's and Larissa's resources similar?
How are they different?

Scenarios

III. Resource Check
List Examples

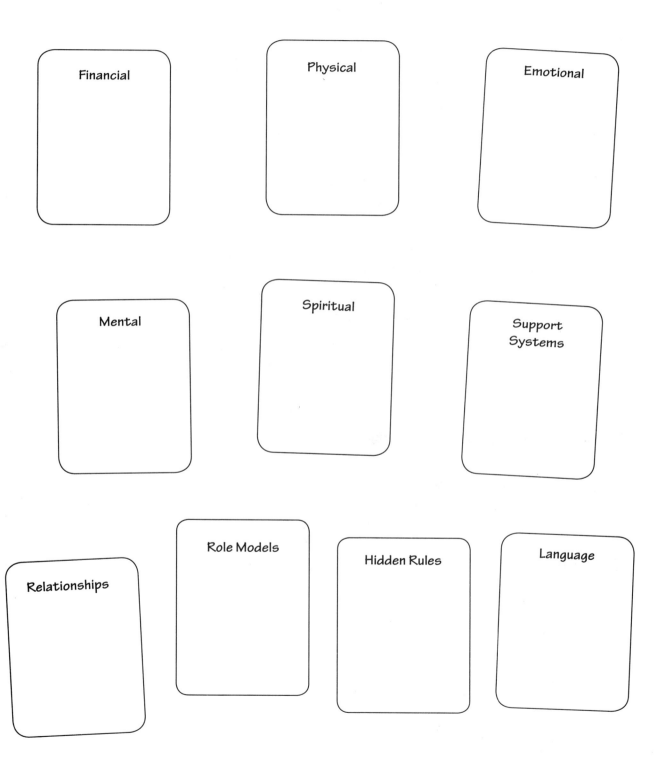

Chapter 3—Resources

IV. Check Your Cards

Rate the level of each resource in your hand relevant to your current and future pictures. Which cards will you add or discard to help you reach your future picture?

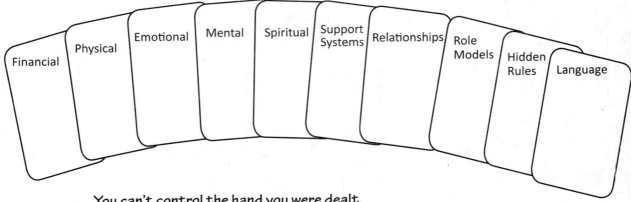

You can't control the hand you were dealt.
You can decide how to play it.

Low: 2 to 5
Medium: 6 to 9
High: 10 to Ace
Lottery: Joker

V. Current and Future Pictures

Pick one resource you want to focus on.
Create a current picture of the resource.
Create a future picture of the resource.
List action steps to get from your current picture to your future picture.

Current Picture   **Future Picture**

VI. A Little Quiz

1. Which resource has the greatest influence on being a lifelong learner?

2. Which resource cannot be purchased?

3. Which resource has the greatest influence on lifelong stability?

4. Which resource has the greatest impact on the success of a student in school?

5. List three personal support systems.

6. What are the benefits of having spiritual resources?

7. JOURNAL ITEM: Which resource is the most important? Why?

VII. Community Resource Project

Review the resources discussed in this chapter.

Work in teams to develop a current picture of resources in your community.
    Note: May be text, a picture, list, graph, data, website review, etc.
Teams complete and present current pictures to the class.

As a class, brainstorm resources that are available in your community.
Create a list and post in the classroom.

As a class, brainstorm resources that are needed but not available in your community.
Create a list and post in the classroom.

Use tools online to research and gather information on local resources including: organizations, clubs, service providers, clinics, educational institutions, transportation, employment office, individuals, etc.

By the end of the year, develop a list of resources in your community that includes contact information, services, locations, hours of operation, etc.

Complete the necessary steps of the review and approval process for distribution.

Post information on the school or community website.

Publish a paper copy. File a copy in personal planners and distribute to local youth.

Research and discuss options to work with other agencies to develop missing resources or bring them to your community.

Your mind is a tool to invent and discover.
Your mind is a weapon to fight fear and injustice.
Your mind is a resource to create the world we all want to live in.

In *The R Rules* ...

Life is like a card game ...
Everyone gets a set of cards.
You can't control the cards you get.
You can decide how to play them.

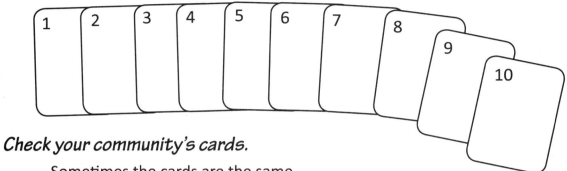

Check your community's cards.
Sometimes the cards are the same.
Sometimes the cards are different.

All communities ...
Have hopes and fears, goals and dreams.
Face unique challenges and situations.
Use the resources available to achieve and win.
Are problem solvers.

1. Financial
2. Physical
3. Emotional
4. Mental
5. Spiritual
6. Support Systems
7. Relationships
8. Role Models
9. Hidden Rules
10. Language

We all ...
1. Live in a particular region or part of a country.
2. Belong to a group or groups based on cultural heritage.
3. Face the possibility of illness or disability.
4. Have intelligence and an education—formal and/or informal.
5. Will experience the effects of aging.
6. Deal with various expectations related to gender.
7. Have an economic reality and are members of an economic class.
8. Use the rules and patterns we know.
9. Have a variety of resources—external and internal.
10. Use languages to communicate and negotiate.

Communities are all different. Communities are all alike.

Chapter 3—Resources

VIII. Social Capital

Capital is a term for resources such as money, property, or networks that represent assets or wealth.

Social capital is the term for having connections to individuals or a community. Two types of social capital are bonding and bridging.

Bonding capital is the term for being connected to those who have the same interests or goals. Examples: members of a team, students in this class, family members.

Bridging capital is the term for being connected to networks outside our normal circle. Examples: community members, an organization.

 Why is social capital an important resource?

List types of social capital.

Discuss mental models or strategies that can be used to remember "rules" in different situations or environments.

An example: Manners are a resource used to build capital. To remember how to set a table correctly, use the 4/5 rule. Any item with four letters is set to the left of the plate. Any item with five letters is set to the right of the plate.

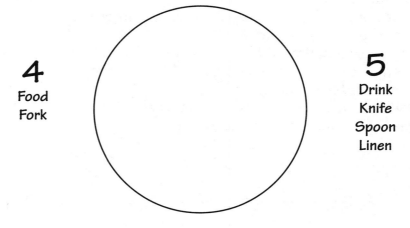

Chapter 3—Resources

IX. 21st Century Skills

The chart below lists resources and skills identified by the Partnership for 21st Century Skills. The mission of the group is to build partnerships between business, education, government, and communities to support the 21st century readiness of students for success.

Log on to http://www.p21.org
Review information on the website, including "Framework for 21st Century Learning."
Below are the 21st century skills and literacies included on the site.

Core Subjects	Communicating and Collaborating
Global Awareness	Information Literacy
Financial and Economic Literacy	Media Literacy
Business and Entrepreneurial Literacy	ICT (Information, Communications, and Technology) Literacy
Civic Literacy	Flexibility and Adaptability
Health Literacy	Initiative and Self-Direction
Environmental Literacy	Social and Cross-Cultural Skills
Creativity and Innovation	Productivity and Accountability
Critical Thinking and Problem Solving	Leadership and Responsibility

- Work with a partner to create a two-minute presentation or a mental model that explains one of the skills or literacies shown in the table above.
- Present to the class. Answer questions and clarify understanding as needed.
- Complete a plus delta evaluation.
- Based on the information presented, identify three of your personal strengths.
- Use the space below to list the three strengths and explain how they will help you enter the workforce and succeed in the 21st century.

 Which of the skills listed above will be needed to complete the community resource project?

IX. 21st Century Skills

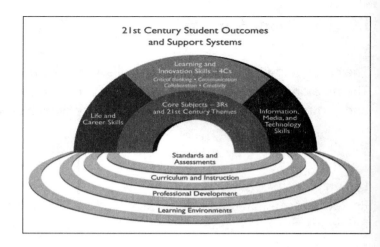

Framework for 21st Century Learning
The Partnership for 21st Century Skills (P21) contains:
Definitions of the P21 framework for student outcomes and support systems
A framework that describes:
> *skills, knowledge, and expertise students must master to succeed in work and life;*
> *it is a blend of content knowledge, specific skills, expertise, and literacies.*

1. Core Subjects
English, Reading, Language Arts   Economics   Government and Civics World Languages   Science   History Arts   Mathematics   Geography
2. 21st Century Themes—woven into core subjects
Global Awareness • Using 21st century skills to understand and access global issues. • Learning from working collaboratively with individuals representing diverse cultures, religions, and lifestyles in a spirit of mutual respect and open dialogue in personal, work, and community contexts. • Understanding other nations and cultures, including the use of non-English languages.
Financial, Economic, Business, and Entrepreneurial Literacy • Knowing how to make appropriate personal economic choices. • Understanding the role of the economy in society. • Using entrepreneurial skills to enhance workplace productivity and career options.
Civic Literacy • Participating effectively in civic life through knowing how to stay informed and understanding governmental processes. • Exercising the rights and obligations of citizenship at local, state, national, and global levels. • Understanding the local and global implications of civic decisions.
Health Literacy • Obtaining, interpreting, and understanding basic health information and services and using such information and services in ways that enhance health. • Understanding preventive physical and mental health measures, including proper diet, nutrition, exercise, risk avoidance, and stress reduction. • Using available information to make appropriate health-related decisions. • Establishing and monitoring personal and family health goals. • Understanding national and international public health and safety issues.

IX. 21st Century Skills

2. 21st Century Themes—woven into core subjects

Environmental Literacy
- Demonstrate knowledge and understanding of the environment and the circumstances and conditions affecting it, particularly as relates to air, climate, land, food, energy, water, and ecosystems.
- Demonstrate knowledge and understanding of society's impact on the natural world (e.g., population growth, population development, resource consumption rate, etc.).
- Investigate and analyze environmental issues and make accurate conclusions about effective solutions.
- Take individual and collective action towards addressing environmental challenges (e.g., participating in global actions, designing solutions that inspire action on environmental issues).

3. Learning and Innovation Skills

Creativity and Innovation
Think Creatively
- Use a wide range of idea creation techniques (such as brainstorming).
- Create new and worthwhile ideas (both incremental and radical concepts).
- Elaborate, refine, analyze, and evaluate own ideas in order to improve and maximize creative efforts.

Work Creatively with Others
- Develop, implement, and communicate new ideas to others effectively.
- Be open and responsive to new and diverse perspectives; incorporate group input and feedback into the work.
- Demonstrate originality and inventiveness in work and understand the real-world limit to adopting new ideas.
- View failure as an opportunity to learn; understand that creativity and innovation are long-term, cyclical processes of small successes and frequent mistakes.

Implement Innovations
- Act on creative ideas to make a tangible and useful contribution to the field in which the innovation will occur.

Critical Thinking and Problem Solving
Reason Effectively
- Use various types of reasoning (inductive, deductive, etc.) as appropriate to the situation.
- Use systems thinking.
- Analyze how parts of a whole interact with each other to produce overall outcomes in complex systems.

Make Judgments and Decisions
- Effectively analyze and evaluate evidence, arguments, claims, and beliefs.
- Analyze and evaluate major alternative points of view.
- Synthesize and make connections between information and arguments.
- Interpret information and draw conclusions based on the best analysis.
- Reflect critically on learning experiences and processes.

Solve Problems
- Solve different kinds of unfamiliar problems in both conventional and innovative ways.
- Identify and ask significant questions that clarify various points of view and lead to better solutions.

Communication and Collaboration
Communicate Clearly
- Articulate thoughts and ideas effectively using oral, written, and nonverbal communication skills in a variety of forms and contexts.
- Listen effectively to decipher meaning, including knowledge, values, attitudes, and intentions.
- Use communication for a range of purposes (e.g., to inform, instruct, motivate, and persuade).
- Utilize multiple media and technologies and know how to judge their effectiveness as well as assess their impact.
- Communicate effectively in diverse environments (including multilingual).

Collaborate with Others
- Demonstrate ability to work effectively and respectfully with diverse teams.
- Exercise flexibility and willingness to be helpful in making necessary compromises to accomplish a common goal.
- Assume shared responsibility for collaborative work and value the individual contributions made by each team member.

IX. 21st Century Skills

4. Information, Media, and Technology Skills—*marked by various characteristics*

Information Literacy
Access and Evaluate Information
- Access information efficiently (time) and effectively (sources).
- Evaluate information critically and competently.

Use and Manage Information
- Use information accurately and creatively for the issue or problem at hand.
- Manage the flow of information from a wide variety of sources.
- Apply a fundamental understanding of the ethical/legal issues surrounding the access and use of information.

Media Literacy
Analyze Media
- Understand both how and why media messages are constructed, and for what purposes.
- Examine how individuals interpret messages differently, how values and points of view are included or excluded, and how media can influence beliefs and behaviors.
- Apply a fundamental understanding of the ethical/legal issues surrounding the access and use of media.

Create Media Products
- Understand and use the most appropriate media creation tools, characteristics, and conventions.
- Understand and effectively use the most appropriate expressions and interpretations in diverse, multicultural environments.

ICT (Information, Communication, and Technology) Literacy
Apply Technology Effectively
- Use technology as a tool to research, organize, evaluate, and communicate information.
- Use digital technologies (computers, smartphones, media players, GPS, etc.), communication/networking tools, and social networks appropriately to access, manage, integrate, evaluate, and create information to successfully function in a knowledge economy.
- Apply a fundamental understanding of the ethical/legal issues surrounding the access and use of information technologies.

5. Life and Career Skills

Flexibility and Adaptability
Adapt to Change
- Adapt to varied roles, job responsibilities, schedules, and contexts.
- Work effectively in a climate of ambiguity and changing priorities.
- Utilize multiple media and technologies and know how to judge their effectiveness as well as assess their impact.

Be Flexible
- Incorporate feedback effectively.
- Deal positively with praise, setbacks, and criticism.
- Understand, negotiate, and balance diverse views and beliefs to reach workable solutions, particularly in multicultural environments.

Social and Cross-Cultural Skills
Interact Effectively with Others
- Know when it is appropriate to listen and when it is appropriate to speak.
- Conduct oneself in a respectable, professional manner.

Work Effectively in Diverse Teams
- Respect cultural differences and work effectively with people from a range of social and cultural backgrounds.
- Respond open-mindedly to different ideas and values.
- Leverage social and cultural differences to create new ideas and increase both innovation and quality of work.

IX. 21st Century Skills

5. Life and Career Skills

Initiative and Self-Direction
  Manage Goals and Time
    • Set goals with tangible and intangible success criteria.
    • Balance tactical (short-term) and strategic (long-term) goals.
    • Use time and manage workload efficiently.
  Work Independently
    • Monitor, define, prioritize, and complete tasks without direct oversight.
  Be a Self-Directed Learner
    • Go beyond basic mastery of skills and/or curriculum to explore and expand one's own learning and opportunities to gain expertise.
    • Demonstrate initiative to advance skill levels towards a professional level.
    • Demonstrate commitment to learning as a lifelong process.
    • Reflect critically on past experiences in order to inform future progress.

Productivity and Accountability
  Manage Projects
    • Set and meet goals, even in the face of obstacles and competing pressures.
    • Prioritize, plan, and manage work to achieve the intended result.
  Produce Results
    • Demonstrate additional attributes associated with producing high-quality products, including the abilities to:
      - Work positively and ethically
      - Manage time and projects effectively
      - Multitask
      - Participate actively, as well as be reliable and punctual
      - Present oneself professionally and with proper etiquette
      - Collaborate and cooperate effectively with teams
      - Respect and appreciate team diversity
      - Be accountable for results

Leadership and Responsibility
  Guide and Lead Others
    • Use interpersonal and problem solving skills to influence and guide others toward a goal.
    • Leverage strengths of others to accomplish a common goal.
    • Inspire others to reach their very best via example and selflessness.
    • Demonstrate integrity and ethical behavior in using influence and power.
  Be Responsible to Others
    • Act responsibly with the interests of the larger community in mind.

X. Plus Delta Evaluation

A process to provide information that can be used to improve presentations and skills and offer different points of view. Process also develops evaluation skills.

+ Plus is the symbol for positive.

▲ Delta is the symbol for change.

1. Write name of presenter and topic or title of presentation.
2. Write name of person evaluating the project.
3. Review criteria and directions for the project.
4. Write comment(s) on what is positive or working.
5. Write comment(s) on what could be changed or improved.
6. Comments should be thoughtful and worded respectfully.
7. Evaluations are completed and turned in to the instructor who will issue grades to both the evaluator and the presenter.

Presenter_____
Topic_____

+ Comment on something that was positive—a plus to the presentation.

▲ Comment on something that could be changed or might improve the presentation.

Rating: 1 2 3 4 5

Evaluator _____

GEAR UP, Farmington Municipal Schools, New Mexico.
Used with permission.

XI. Resources

> "How do you plan on going to college?"
> "By car."

That was the question on a GEAR UP survey and the answer given by a student in the GEAR UP postsecondary preparation program. On first read, I thought the young woman had answered trying to be funny or rude. After investigating, I learned it was neither. Her answer simply stated the plan she had developed to get her to college. The college she was going to attend was 400 miles from her home. Because her family did not have a car, she made arrangements with a friend to drive her to college—by car.

My reaction to the student's answer was based on my personal mental models and resources. Use *The R Rules* to increase understanding of resources and their relevance to relationships, planning, and navigating environments different than your own. Identify and develop resources needed to achieve your future picture.

We use the patterns we know ...

Timothy Lucas, *Schools That Learn: A Fifth Discipline Fieldbook for Educators, Parents, and Everyone Who Cares About Education.* Used with permission.

XI. Resources

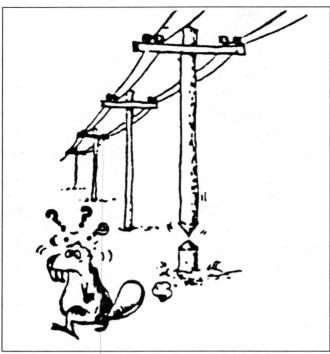

Timothy Lucas, *Schools That Learn: A Fifth Discipline Fieldbook for Educators, Parents, and Everyone Who Cares About Education.* Used with permission.

Under-resourced is defined as not having the resources to address a particular situation or navigate a particular environment.

"Everybody is a genius, but if you judge a fish by its ability to climb a tree, it will spend its entire life believing it is stupid."

– Albert Einstein

XII. R Rules Raffiti

Quotations can inspire and motivate—they are a resource.
Whose words are a resource to you?

> "How wonderful that nobody need wait a single moment before beginning to improve the world." –Anne Frank

XIII. Resources

1. Key Points
2. 10 Resources
3. Resource Check
4. Card Check
5. Little Quiz and Journal
6. Community Resource Project
7. Social Capital
8. 21st Century Skills
9. Plus Delta Evaluation Tool
10. Raffiti, Reflect, Reference

4.0	I understand the chapter and can teach the concepts I learned to others. What I learned is important and can be used in the following ways:
3.0	I understand the chapter and do not have any questions about the concepts. What I learned is important because:
2.0	I understand parts of this chapter. I still don't understand and have questions about:
1.0	I still need help to understand the basic concepts of this chapter. Specifically about:

Action steps for using what I learned in this chapter:

Rubric by K. Dixon

XIII. Resources Definitions, Symbols, Mental Models, Tools

Definitions

Capital: Resources such as money, property, or networks that represent wealth.

Social capital: Having connections to individuals or a community.
Two types of social capital: bridging and bonding.

Bonding capital: Being connected to those who have the same interests or goals.
Examples: members of a team, students in this class.

Bridging capital: Being connected to networks outside our normal circle.

Symbols and Mental Models

  Symbol for positive, what is working

  Greek symbol for change; used to indicate what could be changed or improved

Tool

Plus-Delta

Tool to show what is working or positive and what could be changed or improved.

Step 1: List what is working or having a positive impact under the plus sign.
Step 2: List anything that could be changed or improved under the delta.
Step 3: Write a plan to improve or change the delta items.

Plus +	Delta △

Chapter 3—Resources

Chapter 4 Rules—Learning Objectives

What?	Why?	How?
I. Where Do Rules Come From?	Increase awareness of how information is shared over time and becomes the habits, customs, behaviors, and rules of groups.	Use activities to identify and understand patterns, mental models, self-talk, and generational transfer of knowledge.
II. Hidden Rules	Define, identify, and discuss hidden rules.	Explore hidden rules and examples in various environments.
III. Patterns	*The R Rules* is based on patterns. All patterns have exceptions.	Draw a rooster. Identify and discuss patterns. Use as a mental model.
IV. Patterns and Hidden Rules	Understand and identify patterns and hidden rules relevant to mental models, behaviors, and achievement.	Discuss patterns and hidden rules related to various settings, cultures, school, work, and life.
V. Patterns and Rules	Identify rules and patterns. Analyze research for increased understanding across environments.	Create and use mental models to identify patterns. Explore rules and hidden rules in multiple systems and environments.
VI. R Rules	Review *The R Rules* foundations.	Discussion and review of *The R Rules* foundations.
VII. Key Points	Review and discuss key points to ensure understanding.	Review, discuss, and demonstrate understanding of concepts and applications.
VIII. Raffiti, Rubric, Definitions	Clarify information, reflect, and define mental models.	Build knowledge, resources, and vocabulary.
Check items to be filed in your R Rules Personal Planner.		

Chapter 4—Rules

Every game has rules.
Some rules are written.
Some rules are not.

I. Where do rules come from?

People use the patterns and understandings of the cultures they grow up in. They are passed from generation to generation and over time become the habits, customs, and rules—both written and unwritten—that are the accepted behaviors of the group.

In the chapter on resources, the beaver used the set of rules he grew up with. As he learned, different systems often require different rules and new understandings. Use this chapter to explore rules—written and unwritten—and understand how they influence thinking, behaviors, and success at school, work, and in life.

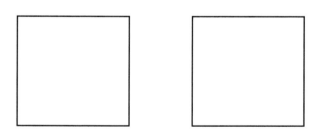

Without looking at an actual coin, draw the front of a penny in the first box, and draw the back of a penny in the second box. Look at a penny. How did you do? Rules and mental models are often at the subconscious level. Like the pennies, they are used every day but often remain unnoticed, or "under the radar."

Look at the diagram on the next page.
Tell a story about what happened.

I. Where do rules come from?

 Experiences are resources we use to understand environments and respond in different situations. We all get a set of cards. Review the cards below. How did each of these cards influence the story you used to explain the tracks on the previous page?

 Experiences—What we know, have done, and remember.

 Mental Models—Images in our mind of how we believe the world is or should be.

 Assumptions—Information or beliefs used without proof they are accurate.

 Habits—Patterns of behaviors that are repeated and done automatically.

 Expectations—What an individual believes will or should happen.

 Realities—What is actual or real, or what an individual believes to be real.

 Beliefs—What individuals accept be true.

 Culture—The shared beliefs and values of a group.

 I see. I hear. ⟶ I tell myself a story. ⟶ I act.

 Check your cards.
Check your self-talk.
What stories do you tell yourself?
What cards will you add? Discard?

Chapter 4—Rules

I. Where do rules come from?

We use stories to share information. Often stories—like the ones above—have been passed from generation to generation. Sometimes the original meaning has been forgotten or has changed over time.

Do you know the hidden meaning, "real story," or
the origin of each of the nursery rhymes pictured?

II. Hidden Rules

We all have family traditions and customs. In our family all of the women cut the ends off of a roast before we cook it. We do this because that is the way our grandmother prepared and cooked her roasts.

This is an example of a "hidden rule." Hidden rules are the unspoken habits and patterns used by a group. They are the rules that have been in place and in use for so long that they have become invisible. "Everyone" knows them; they are automatic. And often the original meaning has been forgotten or has changed over time.

Different environments use different rules, and in order to have a voice there, it is necessary to understand the rules. Since no one tells you the "hidden rules," you may not know they even exist until you break one. You know you've broken a hidden rule when you get the "LOOK." The look—an eye roll, a shoulder shrug, or silence that lets you know you broke a rule. People may assume you are rude or not too bright. Worse yet, unless someone explains the hidden rules and the expectations, it is almost impossible to know what to do differently.

School, work, and home all have their own sets of "hidden rules." Use *The R Rules* to identify and develop resources that support your goals and the results you want in both your current and future pictures.

III. Patterns

The R Rules uses patterns.
Patterns occur most of the time, not every time. *All* patterns have exceptions.
There are different sets of rules and patterns for different systems and environments.
Sketch a rooster.

IV. Patterns and Hidden Rules

True or False:
All high school students need to be "college ready" at graduation.

—Rita Pierson

Your public profile

 Handshakes
What are the rules?

104°

"Sawu Bona"
"Skihona"

Choices
https://www.youtube.com/watch?v=okIPl95DC8c

What are your rules
about wearing a tie?

Traditional Greeting of the Masai Tribe:
    "'How are the children?"

V. Patterns and Rules

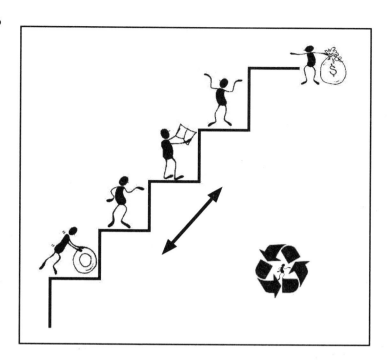

Four Research Patterns
Behavior of the Individual
Capital in the Community
Exploitation
Political and Economic Structures

Low ———————————————— High

A Continuum

V. Patterns and Rules
Life is like a card game ...

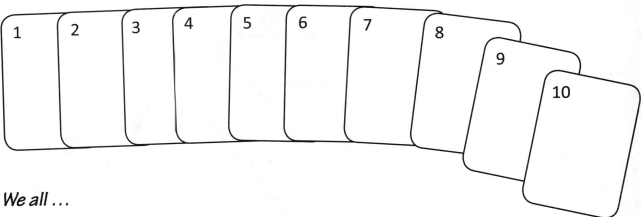

We all ...

1. Live in a particular region or part of a country.
2. Belong to a group or groups based on cultural heritage.
3. Face the possibility of illness or disability.
4. Have intelligence and an education—formal and/or informal.
5. Will experience the effects of aging.
6. Deal with various expectations related to gender.
7. Have an economic reality and are members of an economic class.
8. Use the rules and patterns we know.
9. Have a variety of resources—external and internal.
10. Use languages to communicate and negotiate.

VI. R Rules

To get resources, results, and respect,
understand the rigor, rules, and relationships.

Rules – Relationships = Rebellion
—Grant East

VII. Key Points

If there are different sets of rules, what do you need to know?

1. One set is not any better than another. Every "game" has its own set.
2. Different environments and systems use different rules.
3. Rules are written and unwritten—can be "hidden" and unspoken.
4. To achieve, have a voice, and contribute, learn the rules—both written and unwritten.
5. Rules are relevant to resources, achievement, and safety.
6. *The R Rules* discusses patterns. *All* patterns have exceptions.
7. Individuals use all the rules they know, not just one set. We all "code switch."
8. It is helpful to have someone who is willing to teach and support you as you learn and use new rules and patterns (in relationships of mutual respect).
9. Breaking or using different hidden rules can have a negative impact.
10. Use the information and activities in *The R Rules* to develop resources that will allow you to achieve in your current and future pictures.
11. To have the best schools and communities, we must all work together—we must all have a voice at the table.
12. We are all alike; we are all different.

VIII. R Rules Raffiti
A Pattern

Can you read this? Olny srmat poelpe can.

I cluod not blveiee taht I cluod aulaclty uesdnatnrd waht I was rdanieg. Aoccdrnig to rscheearch at Cmabrigde Uinervtisy, it deosn't mttaer in waht oredr the ltteers in a wrod are; the olny iprmoatnt tihng is taht the frist and lsat ltteer be in the rghit pclae. The rset can be a taotl mses and you can sitll raed it wouthit a porbelm. Tihs is bcuseae the huamn mnid deos not raed ervey lteter by istlef, but the wrod as a wlohe. Amzanig huh? Yaeh, and I awlyas tghuhot slpeling was ipmorantt!

Understanding rules and patterns is a resource.
The ability to "break with limited thinking" is a resource.

Alvin Toffler:
"The illiterate of the 21st century will not be those who cannot read and write, but those who cannot learn, unlearn, and relearn."

What do you need to learn?
What do you need to unlearn?

VIII. Rules

1. Origin of Rules
2. Hidden Rules
3. Patterns
4. R Rules
5. Key Points
6. Raffiti, Reflect, Reference

4.0	I understand the chapter and can teach the concepts I learned to others. What I learned is important and can be used in the following ways:
3.0	I understand the chapter and do not have any questions about the concepts. What I learned is important because:
2.0	I understand parts of this chapter. I still don't understand and have questions about:
1.0	I still need help to understand the basic concepts of this chapter. Specifically about:
My plan for using what I learned in this chapter is:	

Rubric by K. Dixon

VIII. Rules Definitions, Symbols, Mental Models, Tools

Definitions

 Assumptions: Information or beliefs used without proof they are accurate.

 Beliefs: What individuals accept to be true.

 Culture: The shared beliefs and values of a group.

 Expectations: What an individual believes will or should happen.

 Experiences: What we know, have done, and remember.

 Habits: Patterns of behaviors that are repeated and done automatically.

 Mental models: Images in our mind of how we believe the world is or should be.

 Realities: What is actual or real, or what an individual believes to be real.

Breaking with limited thinking: Breaking habits and thinking patterns that limit.

Code-switching: Moving back and forth between two languages; *The R Rules* defines code-switching as the ability to understand and use different rules and behaviors appropriately in different environments.

Continuum: A continuous series that blends together so well it is impossible to say where one part begins or ends.

Generation: Term for time—around 30 years—between the birth of parents and the birth of their children. A group of individuals born and living about the same time with the same interests, ideas, world events, and patterns.

Rooster: Mental model for a pattern and stereotype. All patterns have exceptions. *The R Rules* is based on patterns.

Chapter 5 Realities—Learning Objectives

What?	Why?	How?
I. Realities	Reality is what is believed to be real. Realities change.	View video: "Lost Generation." Review education and earnings.
II. Education and Earnings	Use and analyze data to see patterns related to earnings and education.	Review data on earnings relevant to education and gender.
III. Wants and Needs for One Month	Understand needs and wants, cost of living for one month, relevance of minimum wage.	Clarify needs vs. wants. Identify expenses and budget for one month. Discuss minimum wage.
IV. Finances	Develop resources for financial literacy in various systems.	Utilize tools, seminars, websites, virtual simulations, and guest speakers.
V. Card of Fate	Strategy to solve problems and think critically.	Use scenarios to identify, access, and develop resources.
VI. Today's Reality	Scenarios to develop financial literacy.	Use career cards to understand budget and cost of living.
VII. Career Survey	Increase awareness of career options and interests.	Complete career assessment. Develop R Rules Professional Portfolios.
VIII. States Career Cluster Initiative	Understanding of career clusters, pathways, and programs of study.	Complete survey and activities on career clusters, pathways, and programs of study.
IX. Career Clusters	Activities to apply learning about career clusters.	Identify businesses, break down career clusters, create resume.
X. Online Profiles	Use online resources to increase career choices and readiness.	Develop career profile and research clusters, careers, options.
XI. College Resources	Understand college planning, options, and resources.	Define college, actions to earn diploma and credits. Identify strategies and terms.
XII. College Career Readiness	Increased awareness of college placement exams, National Career Readiness Certification, and interview skills.	Review ACT, COMPASS, SAT, Accuplacer, WorkKeys, and National Career Readiness Certificate. Complete interviews.
XIII. Raffiti, Rubric, Resources	Clarify information, reflect, and define mental models.	Build knowledge, resources, and vocabulary.
Check items to be filed in your R Rules Personal Planner.		

Chapter 5—Realities

I. Reality—What is actual, real, or true, or what an individual believes to be real or true.

Lost Generation—A Reality
https://www.youtube.com/watch?v=42E2fAWM6rA

II. Education and Earnings—A Reality

U.S. Median Income for Persons Age 25 and Older

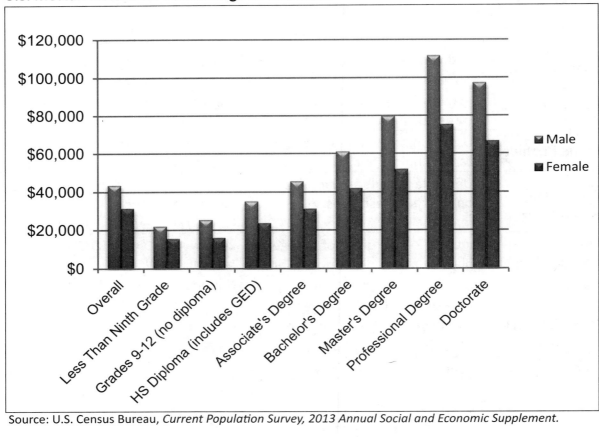

Source: U.S. Census Bureau, *Current Population Survey, 2013 Annual Social and Economic Supplement.*

II. Education and Earnings

A Reality

Level of Education	Annual Earnings	Hourly Earnings
Doctorate	$100,968	$50.00
Professional Degree	$102,240	$51.00
Master's Degree	$77,505	$39.00
Bachelor's Degree	$60,758	$30.00
Associate's Degree	$45,834	$23.00
HS Diploma (GED)	$35,373	$18.00
Grades 9–12 No Diploma	$25,058	$12.00
Less Than Ninth Grade	$21,339	$10.60
Federal Minimum Wage		$7.25

Source: U.S. Census Bureau, *Current Population Survey, 2013 Annual Social and Economic Supplement.*

How much does a high school graduate earn over a lifetime compared to a high school dropout?

How much is every hour you stay in school, from now until you graduate, worth to you in earnings over a lifetime?

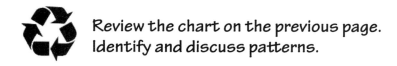

Review the chart on the previous page.
Identify and discuss patterns.

III. Wants and Needs for One Month

CATEGORY	MONTHLY BUDGET	MONTHLY ACTUAL	DIFFERENCE
Rent			
Electricity			
Water and Sewer			
Natural Gas or Oil			
Groceries			
Eating Out, Lunches, Snacks			
Car Payment and Insurance			
Gasoline and Maintenance			
Public Transportation (Bus, Subway)			
Phone			
Laundromat, Dry Cleaners			
Internet, Cable TV, Movies			
Day Care			
Toiletries, Household Products			
Insurance, Medical Expenses			
Clothing			
Grooming (Hair, Makeup)			
Credit Cards			
Savings			
Emergency Fund			
Gifts/Donations			
Miscellaneous Expenses			
Total Monthly Expenses			

Discuss needs vs. wants.

List amounts for each expense.
1. First column: Answer based on personal experience or estimate.
2. Second column: Answer based on research.
   a. Use Internet, newspaper, or contact service providers to determine actual cost.
   b. Compare phone, Internet, and cable plans.
   c. Create a grocery list and go to the store to get an actual total.

III. How Much Do You Need?

Budgets are mental models—a picture of how money is being spent. Use a budget to see patterns, predict, and plan.

CATEGORY	EARNINGS	EXPENSES	BALANCE
INCOME:			
Wages 40 hours x $7.25 x 4			
40 hours x $10.60 x 4	$1,696.00		$1,696.00
40 hours x $12.00 x 4	$1,920.00		$1,920.00
TAXES WITHHELD:			
FICA			
Federal			
State			
Medicare			
NET INCOME:			
EXPENSES:			
Disposable Income:			

Research and discuss minimum wage and average hourly wages in your area. Brainstorm and discuss options that could make your money go farther.

Repeat the activity using the average pay rate earned by a high school graduate. Does this show you a different reality for earning a high school diploma or working toward technical certification or an associate's degree while attending or after high school?

Challenge:
What is your opinion on raising the minimum wage?
Respond as an employer and employee.
Justify your answer.

Check out and discuss:
http://www.dol.gov/whd/minwage/america.htm
The department of labor in your state.

Chapter 5—Realities

IV. Finances

1. Build resources to reach your future picture.
    Financial expert Dave Ramsey says, "Spend on paper; spend with purpose."

    Use mental models - A written budget to predict, review, and plan.
                       - Planning backwards, organizers, force field diagrams.
    What, why, how   - Define needs and wants.
                       - Identify what is important to you and why.
                       - Note patterns and use them to monitor and make revisions.

2. Create and use an envelope tool.

    ## The Envelope Tool
    Budget
    Research Paper
    College Search
    Job Search
    Create a Resume

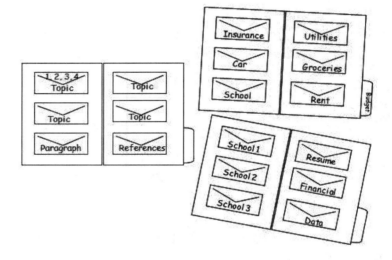

3. View and discuss:

    ✋ Khan Academy
    Review website thoroughly; identify and take notes on resources available.
    Locate Economics and Finance section and review.
    Take notes on:
    Interest and Debt, Taxes, and *Entrepreneurship.*
    https://www.khanacademy.org

    ✋ Practical Money Skills for Life
    Money Matters: College, Cell Phone, Car
    https://www.practicalmoneyskills.com/foreducators/lesson_plans/lev9-12/SA_Lesson1.pdf
    Credit Cards
    https://www.practicalmoneyskills.com/foreducators/lesson_plans/lev_4/L4Activities5.pdf

IV. Finances

4. Invite guest speakers from local financial institutions and businesses to visit your classroom and provide information on the following:
   - Checking Accounts
   - Savings Accounts
   - Credit Cards
   - Debit Cards
   - Processes for Obtaining a Loan
   - Credit Reports
   - Debt Options
   - Purchasing a Car
   - *Information on topics you want to know about*

5. Virtual Learning
   - https://www.practicalmoneyskills.com/games/
     Write a review of one of the games on this site.
     Include a rating for (1) information provided and (2) entertainment value.

   - Make virtual investments.
     Create an investment log (spreadsheet).
     Determine the amount of money that will be used for your initial investment.
     Research stocks to determine stocks you will purchase, or use a random draw.
     Enter information in log: stock value, number of stocks, total investment, etc.
     Monitor stock prices weekly; update or revise your investment log.
     Invite members of your local financial community to speak on this topic.

Date	Stock Name	Stock Symbol	Share Value	Number of Shares	Current Value	Previous Value	Change in Value

V. Card of Fate

ASK: What, Why, How

1. What is the current situation?
   Is this a pattern?

2. Is this important? Why?
   How is this relevant to my current or future picture?

3. Do I need to respond? Why?
   How much time do I have before I respond?

4. What is the best way to respond? Why?
   What are my options?

5. What resources do I need?
   Do I have the resources?
   How can I get these resources?
   What resources could I use instead?

6. What or who can provide information, support, or advice?

VI. Today's Reality

 Play the cards you are dealt.

CATEGORY	+	−	BALANCE
Your Gross Monthly Income			
Spouse's Gross Monthly Income			
Wages and Bonuses			
TOTAL GROSS INCOME			
FICA/Medicare/Social Security			
Federal Income Tax			
State and Local Tax			
401(k) or Retirement			
Union or Professional Dues			
TOTAL NET INCOME			
Mortgage or Rent			
Homeowners/Renters Insurance			
Property Taxes			
Natural Gas			
Electricity			
Water and Sewer			
Television, Entertainment			
Telephone (Land Line, Cell)			
Automobile			
Automobile Expense, Insurance			
Insurance, Medical			
Food			
Childcare			
Student Loans			
Credit Cards			
Pets			
Clothing			
Toiletries, Household Products			
Gifts/Donations			
Travel			

VI. Today's Reality
Careers

What shoes will you wear?

Nine Steps for Planning

1. Assess your personal interests, values, skills, talents, and resources.

2. Review you future picture; consider what you want to do, be, or have and why.

3. Evaluate what jobs are projected to be available in the future, requirements for those jobs, and where the jobs are located.

4. Look at specific jobs that are available now, and research two companies you are interested in working for.

5. Conduct a school search to determine what colleges offer courses or majors you will need.

6. Check with your counselor for information on advanced placement, dual credit, online courses, early college options, and opportunities to shadow.

7. Talk to someone who has a job you want or has attended a school you are interested in.

8. Visit the school or company that you are interested in.

9. Update your future picture; create and use a plan of study and an action plan to reach your goal.

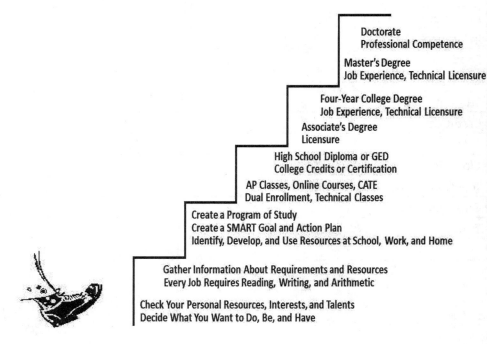

VII. Career Survey ... How Well Do You Know Yourself?

1. In each section below, read and check all the items that apply to you.
2. Total the number of items checked in each section.
3. Write the total in the box for each career path at bottom of each section.
4. Complete and total.
5. Go to the chart of occupations on pages 126–127.
6. Review each occupation group and use information to help you determine priorities and make choices.

ACTIVITIES THAT SOUND INTERESTING	ACTIVITIES THAT SOUND INTERESTING
_1. Reading or writing stories or articles	_1. Interviewing people
_2. Designing and building scenery for plays	_2. Using computer programs
_3. Taking photographs	_3. Winning a sales contest
_4. Acting in a play or movie	_4. Being captain/leader of a team
_5. Listening to/playing music	_5. Working with numbers
_6. Designing clothing, brochures, or posters	_6. Dealing with money
MY PERSONAL QUALITIES	**MY PERSONAL QUALITIES**
_1. Imaginative	_1. Practical
_2. Creative	_2. Independent
_3. Outgoing	_3. Organized
_4. Expressive	_4. Leader
_5. Performer	_5. Like to be around people
IN MY FREE TIME I WOULD ENJOY	**IN MY FREE TIME I WOULD ENJOY**
_1. Working on the school paper or yearbook	_1. Being in a speech contest or debate
_2. Acting in a play or video	_2. Surfing the Internet
_3. Painting pictures, murals, and drawing	_3. Designing a website
_4. Broadcasting a sporting event	_4. Starting my own business
SCHOOL SUBJECTS AND ACTIVITIES I ENJOY AND DO WELL IN	**SCHOOL SUBJECTS AND ACTIVITIES I ENJOY AND DO WELL IN**
_1. Social Studies	_1. Speech
_2. Choir, Symphony, Band	_2. Language
_3. Creative Writing	_3. Math
_4. Art	_4. Marketing
_5. Drama	_5. Accounting
_6. Drafting	_6. Technology
_7. Public Speaking	_7. Business Math
TOTAL NUMBER CHECKED CAREER PATH 1 ☐	**TOTAL NUMBER CHECKED CAREER PATH 2** ☐

Survey (as adapted from Career Partnership, Illinois) reprinted with permission from Marie Schumacher.

VII. Career Survey ... How Well Do You Know Yourself?

In each section below, read and check all the items that apply to you.
Total the number of items checked in each section.
Write the total for each section in the box next to the path number.

ACTIVITIES THAT SOUND INTERESTING
_1. Preparing medicine in a pharmacy
_2. Helping sick people
_3. Working with animals
_4. Helping with sports injuries
_5. Studying anatomy and diseases
_6. Performing surgery

MY PERSONAL STRENGTHS
_1. Compassionate and caring
_2. Good listener
_3. Good at following directions carefully
_4. Conscientious and careful
_5. Patient

IN MY FREE TIME I WOULD ENJOY
_1. Volunteering at a hospital or senior home
_2. Taking care of pets
_3. Exercising and taking care of myself
_4. Working as a trainer on a team

**SCHOOL SUBJECTS AND ACTIVITIES
I ENJOY AND DO WELL IN**
_1. Math
_2. Science
_3. Biology
_4. Chemistry
_5. Communication
_6. Spanish/French
_7. Health

TOTAL NUMBER CHECKED CAREER PATH 3 [   ]

ACTIVITIES THAT SOUND INTERESTING
_1. Helping people solve problems
_2. Working with children
_3. Working with elderly people
_4. Preparing food
_5. Being involved in politics
_6. Solving a mystery

MY PERSONAL QUALITIES
_1. Friendly
_2. Outgoing
_3. Good at making decisions
_4. Good listener
_5. Follow directions

IN MY FREE TIME I WOULD ENJOY
_1. Helping solve my friends' problems
_2. Helping on a community project
_3. Coaching/tutoring
_4. Exploring new places

**SCHOOL SUBJECTS AND ACTIVITIES
I ENJOY AND DO WELL IN**
_1. Language Arts
_2. History
_3. Speech
_4. Math

TOTAL NUMBER CHECKED CAREER PATH 4 [   ]

Survey (as adapted from Career Partnership, Illinois) reprinted with permission from Marie Schumacher.

VII. Career Survey ... How Well Do You Know Yourself?

In each section below, read and check all the items that apply to you.
Total the number of items checked in each section.
Write the total for each section in the box next to the path number.

ACTIVITIES THAT SOUND INTERESTING	ACTIVITIES THAT SOUND INTERESTING
_1. Putting things together	_1. Being outdoors
_2. Designing buildings	_2. Predicting and measuring earthquakes
_3. Working on cars/mechanical things	_3. Growing flowers, plants, and/or trees
_4. Using advanced math to solve problems	_4. Studying rocks and minerals
_5. Fixing things that are broken	_5. Raising fish or animals
_6. Using tools	_6. Working in a chemistry lab
MY PERSONAL QUALITIES	**MY PERSONAL QUALITIES**
_1. Practical	_1. Curious
_2. Like using my hands	_2. Nature lover
_3. Logical	_3. Physically active
_4. Good at reading manuals	_4. Problem solver
_5. Observant	_5. Sense of direction
IN MY FREE TIME I WOULD ENJOY	**IN MY FREE TIME I WOULD ENJOY**
_1. Building models	_1. Camping
_2. Drawing car prototypes	_2. Going on a nature trail
_3. Designing mechanical things	_3. Experimenting with a chemistry set
_4. Inventing a new product	_4. Mountain climbing
SCHOOL SUBJECTS AND ACTIVITIES I ENJOY AND DO WELL IN	**SCHOOL SUBJECTS AND ACTIVITIES I ENJOY AND DO WELL IN**
_1. Math	_1. Math
_2. Geometry	_2. Biology
_3. Woodworking	_3. Geography
_4. Science	_4. Geometry
_5. Welding	_5. Physics
	_6. Horticulture
TOTAL NUMBER CHECKED CAREER PATH 5 ☐	**TOTAL NUMBER CHECKED CAREER PATH 6** ☐

Survey (as adapted from Career Partnership, Illinois) reprinted with permission from Marie Schumacher.

VII. Career Survey

Write your scores for each section in the box with the same number below.
Use your scores to prioritize your interests.
Draw a line through occupations in each group that do not interest you.
Review occupations in each group that interest you, and do additional research.

1. ARTS AND COMMUNICATIONS
Occupations in this path are related to the humanities and performing, visual, literary, and media arts. These may include: architecture, interior design, creative writing, fashion design, film, fine arts, graphic design and production, journalism, languages, radio, television, advertising, and public relations.

2. BUSINESS, MANAGEMENT, AND COMPUTER TECHNOLOGY
Occupations in this path are related to the business environment. These may include: entrepreneurship, sales, marketing, computer/information systems, finance, accounting, personnel, economics, and management.

3. HEALTH SERVICES
Occupations in this path are related to the promotion of health and the treatment of disease. These may include: research, prevention, treatment, and related technologies.

4. HUMAN SERVICES
Occupations in this path are related to economic, political, and social systems. These may include: education, government, law and law enforcement, leisure and recreation, delivery services, the military, religion, childcare, social services, and personal services.

5. ENGINEERING AND INDUSTRIAL TECHNOLOGY
Occupations in this path are related to the technologies necessary to design, develop, install, and maintain physical systems. These may include: engineering, manufacturing, construction, and related technologies.

6. NATURAL RESOURCES AND ENVIRONMENTAL SCIENCES
Occupations in this path are related to agriculture, the environment, and natural resources. They may include: agricultural sciences, earth science, environmental sciences, fisheries, forestry, horticulture, and wildlife.

What shoes will you wear?
Check your cards and your future picture.
What cards do you need to add?

VIII. States Career Cluster Initiative

In 1996 the Department of Education divided the world of work into 16 groups called career clusters. Clusters were made up of occupations in the same field that required similar knowledge and skills. Each cluster includes occupations from entry level to professional. This process and these 16 groups became the States Career Cluster Initiative.

Career Cluster
Broad grouping of occupations in the same field that require similar knowledge and skills.
Career cluster examples: *agriculture, food,* and *natural resources.*
Career clusters are broken into smaller groups of occupations called career pathways.

Career Pathways
Smaller groupings of jobs in a career cluster that are used to narrow the courses and training necessary to prepare for a particular occupation. Pathways are used as a "path" or sequence of courses in order to earn certificates and degrees.
Career pathway examples:
1. Agriculture Communication
2. Agri-Business and Management
3. Animal Science
4. Agriculture Power Structures Technology
5. Food Products and Processing
6. Natural Resources and Environmental Science
7. Plant and Soil Science

Programs of Study
Specific plans of recommended academic and technical coursework. Individual plans are developed and customized. Programs of study are aligned over several years, starting in high school, in order to prepare students for a particular occupation or career.

Go to the websites below for additional information and examples:
http://www.okcareertech.org/educators
http://cte.dpi.wi.gov/cte_careerclustershome
Your state's department of education website
Your state's department of labor website

Chapter 5—Realities

VIII. The 16 Career Clusters

Agriculture, Food & Natural Resources	The production, processing, marketing, distribution, financing, and development of agricultural commodities and resources including food, fiber, wood products, natural resources, horticulture, and other plant and animal products/resources.
Architecture & Construction	Careers in designing, planning, managing, building, and maintaining the built environment.
Arts, A/V Technology & Communications	Designing, producing, exhibiting, performing, writing, and publishing multimedia content including visual and performing arts and design, journalism, and entertainment services.
Business, Management & Administration	Planning, organizing, directing, and evaluating business functions essential to efficient and productive business operations. Business management and administration career opportunities are available in every sector of the economy.
Education & Training	Planning, managing, and providing education, training, and related learning support services.
Finance	Services for financial and investment planning, banking, insurance, and business financial management.
Government & Public Administration	Executing governmental functions that include governance, national security, foreign service, planning, revenue and taxation, regulation, and management and administration at the local, state, and federal levels.
Health Science	Planning, managing, and providing therapeutic services, diagnostic services, health informatics, support services, and biotechnology research and development.
Hospitality & Tourism	Hospitality and tourism encompasses the management, marketing, and operations of restaurants and other food services, lodging, attractions, recreation events, and travel related services.
Human Services	Preparing individuals for employment in career pathways that relate to families and human needs.
Information Technology	Building linkages in IT occupations builds a framework for entry-level, technical, and professional careers related to the design, development, support, and management of hardware, software, multimedia, and systems integration services.

VIII. The 16 Career Clusters

Law, Public Safety, Corrections & Security	Planning, managing, and providing legal, public safety, and protective services, and homeland security, including professional and technical support services.
Manufacturing	Planning, managing, and performing the processing of materials into intermediate or final products and related professional and technical support activities such as production planning and control, maintenance, and manufacturing/process engineering.
Marketing, Sales & Service	Planning, managing, and performing marketing activities to reach organizational objectives.
Science, Technology, Engineering & Mathematics	Planning, managing, and providing scientific research and professional and technical services (e.g., physical science, social science, engineering), including laboratory and testing services and research and development services.
Transportation, Distribution & Logistics	Planning, management, and movement of people, materials, and goods by road, pipeline, air, rail, and water and related professional and technical support services, such as transportation infrastructure planning and management, logistics services, mobile equipment, and facility maintenance.
	The career clusters icons are being used with permission of the States' Career Clusters Initiative, 2007, www.careerclusters.org

Check your current and future pictures
against the pathway you are on.
Revise and reroute as needed.

IX. Career Clusters

Use lotus diagrams to explore and gather information related to career clusters.
1. In the center square of Lotus 1, list a career cluster that interests you.
   In each of the additional squares in Lotus 1, list careers in this cluster that you would like to know more about.
   Identify three careers that are of most interest to you in this cluster.
   Write one of these three careers in the center square of Lotus 2.
2. List jobs associated with this career in the additional squares in Lotus 2.
   Identify three of these jobs that most interest you.
3. Write one of these three jobs in the center square of Lotus 3.
   List duties associated with this job in the additional squares in Lotus 3.
4. Complete the same process for the other two careers you selected.
5. Compare all information and file in your planner. Use to develop a future picture, next-step plan, or program of study.

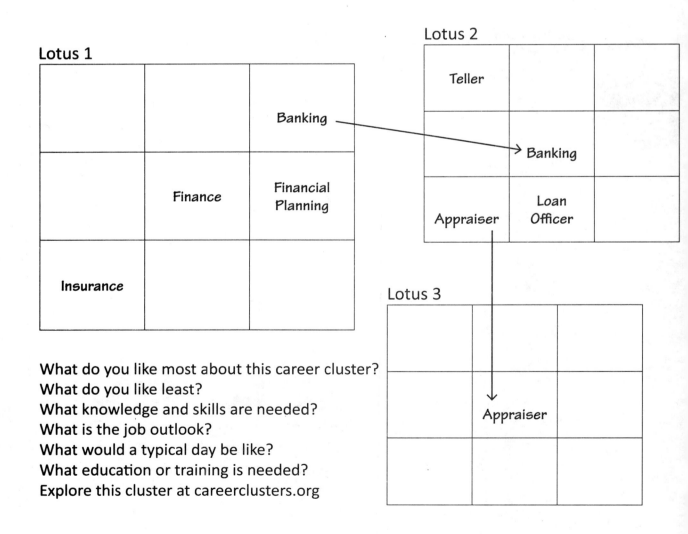

What do you like most about this career cluster?
What do you like least?
What knowledge and skills are needed?
What is the job outlook?
What would a typical day be like?
What education or training is needed?
Explore this cluster at careerclusters.org

IX. Career Clusters

IX. Career Clusters

In the table below, list one business or industry in your community from each of the 16 career clusters.

1.
2.
3.
4.
5.
6.
7.
8.
9.
10.
11.
12.
13.
14.
15.
16.

Challenge:
Identify all of the career clusters that would be represented in a large airport, hospital, or university. Give an example of a job from each cluster.

IX. Career Clusters

Use this table to record work and service experiences.
Translate into language that can be used on a resume or application.

Mowing the yard each week.	Lawn care service and maintenance.

IX. Career Clusters

Identify your interests and begin in a career cluster.
Develop and follow a program of study in high school and college.
Take dual-credit classes or college classes while you are in high school.
Start at entry level and earn while you learn.

A Career Ladder

To work as a clinical laboratory scientist ↑

Next step medical laboratory technician ↑

Start as a phlebotomist/laboratory assistant ↑

See examples of career ladders at:
http://www.careeronestop.org/CompetencyModel/CareerPathway/CPWReviewSamplePaths.aspx

X. Online Profiles

Review the following websites, take notes, explore thoroughly, and use information to develop personal resources. File information in your personal planner and professional portfolio.

A. Go to mynextmove.org

1. Click on the "Interests" tab.
   Complete the O*Net Interest Profiler.
   Print and file the profile results in your personal planner.
2. Return to the mynextmove.org home page and investigate information there, including:
   - A. Bright outlook occupations
   - B. Registered apprenticeships
   - C. Green jobs
   - D. Career search by keyword
   - E. Browse careers by industry

B. Go to www.dws.state.nm.us/careersolutions

1. Select the "Assessments" tab; complete assessments and record your scores for:
   - A. Interest Profiler – Occupation Interest Profiler
   - B. Work Values – Work Importance Locator
   - C. Work Keys – WorkKeys
   - D. Filter Jobs by Characteristic – Beyond Assessments
2. Select the "Job Hunting" tab and review "The Basics."
3. Select "Pocket Resume" from the "Steps" menu. Use information and examples to create your own pocket resume.

C. Review future picture.

Use the information to update your personal planner and professional portfolio.

XI. College Resources

What does college mean to you?
Define college.

What is your reality about going to college?
What can you do now?

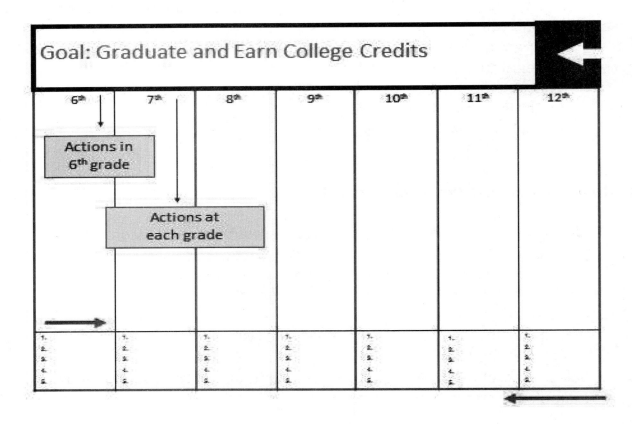

College Tours Online and Campus Visits
Guest Speakers
Advanced Placement Courses
Dual-Credit Courses
Online Courses
Early College High School

XI. College Resources

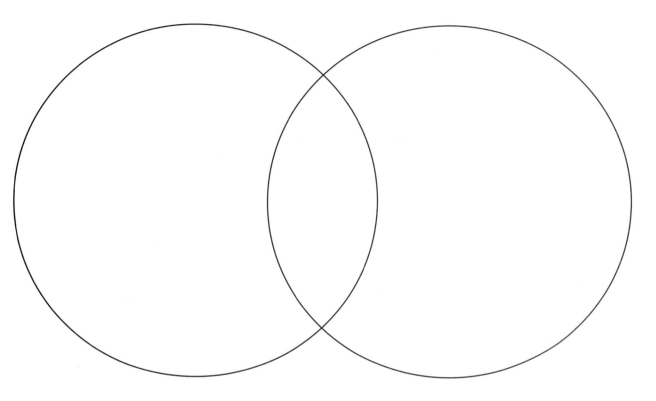

Compare college and high school.
How are they different? How are they alike?

How are the following similar?
How are they different?

GED and High School Diploma
Certification, Licensure, and Degree
Community College and University
Private College and Public College
Scholarship, Grant, Loan

XI. College Resources
Ask: What, Why, How

1. Complete a virtual tour of:
   a. An in-state college or university
   b. A community college
   c. An out-of-state college or university
   d. An online college or university
   e. A career and technical college

2. Take notes during tours that include:
   a. Type of college
   b. Accreditation
   c. Location
   d. Housing
   e. Programs and degrees offered
   f. Admission requirements and process
   g. Costs: tuition, housing, meal plan, books, fees
   h. Financial resources, assistance, scholarships
   i. Students enrolled
   j. Class sizes
   k. Technology
   l. Library
   m. Health center
   n. Cafeteria
   o. Transportation
   p. Any fact or specific feature that is of interest to you

3. Explore these two websites thoroughly to find information that is relevant to achieving your future picture.
   www.collegeboard.org
   www.actstudent.org

   Record information, review, and discuss in class.
   Complete reflection activity.

XI. College Resources

4. Create a future picture of college.

   a. Written paragraph: "Why I want to go to college."
   b. Create a "college wall" in your classroom—include logos.
   c. Create a future picture of *your* college dorm room.
   d. Obtain a course catalog from the college of your choice and create your class schedule for your first year.

5. Visit college campuses.
   a. Review the campus map before tour to locate schools, departments, programs, and to access resources. Identify patterns and use them to plan.
   b. Visit schools and departments that are relevant to your future picture.
   c. Identify career ladders and lattices.
   d. Complete the application process.

6. Invite college students to speak to your class.
   a. Invite graduates from your school who are currently attending college to share their experiences and insights on your campus or via electronic conference.
   b. Talk to students who attend or have attended schools of interest to you.

7. Game day!
   a. College Bingo
   b. College Jeopardy
   c. Concentration
   d. Name That College

8. Schedule conference.
   a. Planner and portfolio checklist

XII. College and Career Readiness

College
Familiarize yourself with college readiness and placement assessments:

    ACT   http://www.actstudent.org/
    _{ACT, EXPLORE, and PLAN}
    COMPASS   http://www.act.org/compass/sample
    SAT   https://www.collegeboard.org/
    ACCUPLACER http://accuplacer.collegeboard.org/students

Career
WorkKeys is a job skills assessment used by employers to assess and hire workers. Learn how you can earn a National Career Readiness Certificate.

1. Go to ACT WorkKeys: https://www.act.org/workkeys/assess/sample.html
2. Click on the following categories and answer the sample questions:
   - Applied Mathematics
   - Reading for Information
   - Locating Information
   - Applied Technology
   - Business Writing
   - Listening for Understanding
   - Teamwork
   - Workplace Observation
   - Fit
   - Performance
   - Talent

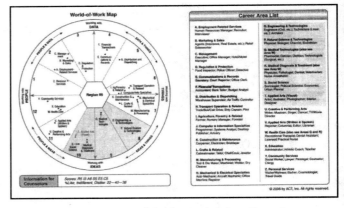

Use ACT World of Work Map Results

Review and update your personal planner.
Review and revise four-year plans and/or programs of study as needed.

R Rules Career Readiness

Name

12 Skills Critical to Job Success

0	.5	1	1.5	2	2.5	3	3.5	4	
									• Applied Mathematics
									• Reading for Information
									• Locating Information
									• Applied Technology
									• Business Writing
									• Listening
									• Teamwork
									• Workplace Observation
									• Writing
									• Fit
									• Performance
									• Talent

R^U Progress Check developed by K. Dixon and B. Souther.
Adapted from ACT WorkKeys.

XII. College and Career Readiness
Resources for an Interview

Dress
Basic interview wardrobe should be fairly conservative and appropriate for the field you will be interviewing in. Consider the type of job, location, and hidden rules.
For most interviews a white blouse or shirt with a collar and a dark skirt or slacks is appropriate.
Fit of clothing is important.
Shoes should be polished, clean.

Language
Use formal register and language of the vocation.
Manners: handshake, please, thank you, yes sir, address interviewer as Mr. or Ms.
Avoid negative comments about past employers.
Check voice, body language, eye contact, posture, etc.

Prepare
Locate information about the company or school—mission, purpose, policies, accomplishments.
Complete online job application; include a hard copy in professional portfolio.
Professional portfolio given to interviewer—contains resume, application, and a business card with contact information.
Practice interviewing with a businessperson, parent, or peer outside of or during class—see questions on following page.
Review strategies you can use if you get nervous; for example, looking up to disengage emotions.

Interview Rubric
1. Applicant was properly dressed.	1 2 3 4 5
2. Applicant shook hands.	1 2 3 4 5
3. Applicant brought R Rules Professional Portfolio.	1 2 3 4 5
4. Applicant used formal register.	1 2 3 4 5
5. Applicant spoke clearly and answered questions concisely.	1 2 3 4 5
6. Applicant used proper body language and maintained eye contact.	1 2 3 4 5
7. Applicant exhibited self-confidence.	1 2 3 4 5
8. Applicant was enthusiastic and ready to begin work.	1 2 3 4 5

Self-Evaluation
What do you think you did well during the interview?
What do you need to improve or practice?
What did you learn about yourself, and what did you learn about an interview?
Would you hire yourself on the basis of your interview?
What will you change for your next interview?

Adapted from the work of Teri Owen and Christine Sterton.

XII. College and Career Readiness
Resources for an Interview

Consider questions that may be asked during an interview.
Use the questions below to practice and discuss possible answers.

1. Tell me about yourself.
2. Why are you interested in this job or school?
3. What are your qualifications for this job?
4. How will your past jobs or experiences be of benefit if you are hired for this job?
5. What are your strengths? What are your weaknesses?
6. What are your career goals?
7. What is your work style? For example, do you prefer to work alone or as a member of a team?
8. Why are you interested in this job?
9. Why should we hire you?
10. What makes you the best candidate for this job?
11. Do you have any questions you would like to ask us?
12. Where do you see yourself in five years?
13. What else would you like us to know that we have not asked?
Others ...

Design your business card here:

XIII. R Rules Raffiti

Would you rather have $100 or
a penny that doubles in value every day for 30 days?

XIII. Realities

1. Lost Generation
2. Education and Earnings
3. Budgets and Financial Activities
4. Card of Fate
5. Today's Reality
6. Career Clusters
7. College Resources
8. College and Career Readiness
9. Raffiti, Reflect, Reference

4.0	I understand the chapter and can teach the concepts I learned to others. What I learned is important and can be used in the following ways:	
3.0	I understand the chapter and do not have any questions about the concepts. What I learned is important because:	
2.0	I understand parts of this chapter. I still don't understand and have questions about:	
1.0	I still need help to understand the basic concepts of this chapter. Specifically about:	

I will use the information in this chapter to support my goals by:

ubric by K. Dixon

XIII. Realities Definitions, Symbols, Mental Models, Tools

Definitions

Reality: What is actual, real, or true, or what an individual believes to be real or true.

Symbols and Mental Models

Tool

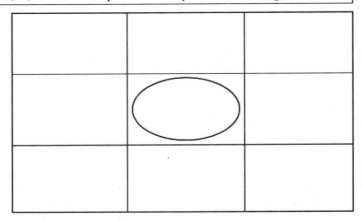

Tool to show parts of the whole and sort and expand information related to a topic or event.

Step 1: Write a topic in the middle box.
Step 2: In each box surrounding the topic, list one related item.
Step 3: Each related item then becomes the topic of a new lotus diagram.
Step 4: The related item goes in the center of the new lotus as a new topic.
Step 5: List categories related to the new topic in each surrounding box.
Step 6: Continue steps 3, 4, and 5 until you have explored all categories.

Chapter 6 Register—Learning Objectives

What?	Why?	How?
I. Register Review	Assess understanding of the five registers of language.	Give an example of each register.
II. Language Relevant to Current and Future Pictures	Understand relevance of language to current and future picture. Increase awareness of regional differences and dialects.	Identify and discuss language needed for current picture and future pictures. Language and words as a resource.
III. SAFE Standard American Formal English	Mental model for language in different settings (e.g., formal register at school and work).	Check for understanding; practice translating from one register to another.
IV. Patterns and Story Structure	There are specific patterns and story structures for formal and casual register.	Discuss patterns and story structures; practice translation activities.
V. Real-Life Applications	Use formal register to respond and communicate in real-life situations.	Respond to interview questions; write and mail a thank you note.
VI. Sentence Structure in Formal Register and Summarizing	Formal register has a specific sentence structure. Understand how to summarize in casual register.	Learn formal register sentence structure and summarizing techniques.
VII. Vocabulary	Assessments use textbook or technical terms. Strategies increase skills. Procedural language impacts achievement. Word walls are a tool to increase vocabulary.	Use vocabulary strategies to learn academic and technical terms and develop study and question making skills. Identify procedural and declarative terms. Use word walls.
VIII. Game Days!	Create and play games to build academic and social skills.	Use games to identify and develop resources.
IX. Raffiti, Rubric, Resources	Clarify information, reflect, and define mental models.	Build knowledge, resources, and vocabulary.
Check items to be filed in your R Rules Personal Planner.		

Chapter 6—Register

Kids Make Nutritious Snacks

Infant Abducted from Hospital Safe

Include Your Children when Baking Cookies

✓ I. Register Review

Write an example in the chart below for each register.

Register	Explanation	
	Frozen	
	Formal	
	Consultative	
	Casual	
	Intimate	

From the work of Joos and Payne.

"The limits of my language are the limits of my mind;
all I know is what I have words for."
—Ludwig Wittgenstein

II. What is the relevance of language to your current and future picture?

Do you have words to communicate ideas and emotions?

Do you know the "hidden rules" of language in different systems and situations?

 American Tongues
—We all live in a particular region or part of the country.

III. SAFE—Standard American Formal English

Two rights, one left.
Stop that.
I won!
You signed the contract.
This eraser sucks!

School and work use formal register.
You may be asked to translate what you said into formal register.

Translations PLEASE!

This is stupid.	
Okay, honey.	
	Please excuse me.
Whatever.	
	I would like to set up an appointment.
That is sick!	

Translate from formal to casual <u>without</u> changing the meaning:
I pledge allegiance to the flag of the United States of America, and to the republic for which it stands, one nation under God, indivisible, with liberty and justice for all.

_____

_____

_____

_____

III. SAFE—Standard American Formal English

Translate to formal register:

> MR DUCKS
> MR NOT DUCKS
> MR 2 DUCKS
> C M WANGS
> LIB MR DUCKS

Translate the underlined words into casual register

<u>We went</u> to the <u>store</u> in our <u>car</u>. As we were <u>driving</u> we <u>saw</u> <u>people</u> at the <u>school</u> moving <u>things</u> on the field. When we <u>got</u> to the <u>store</u> we <u>saw</u> <u>a woman</u> who used to <u>live</u> <u>by</u> us. We <u>said</u> <u>hello</u> and went into the <u>store</u> to <u>buy</u> things.
Adapted from D. Paynter, McREL.

_____

_____

_____

_____

_____

Translate into words.
Work with a partner.
Give directions in words—to the library, office, or gym—without using "nonverbal assists" (pointing, gestures, drawing, or electronics).

From "Jabberwocky" by Lewis Carroll

> 'Twas brillig, and the slithy toves
> Did gyre and gimble in the wabe;
> All mimsy were the borogoves,
> And the mome raths outgrabe.
>
> "Beware the Jabberwock, my son!
> The jaws that bite, the claws that catch!
> Beware the Jubjub bird, and shun
> The frumious Bandersnatch!"

IV. Patterns and Story Structure

Registers:

FROZEN
FORMAL
CONSULTATIVE
CASUAL
INTIMATE

Discourse Patterns:

FORMAL

Let's get down to business.

CASUAL

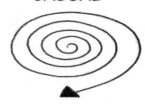

Let's visit.

Story Structure

1. Formal

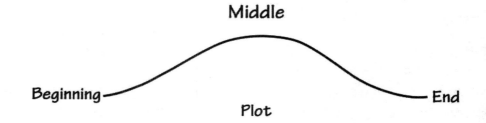

2. Casual

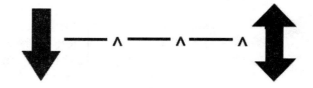

Characterization

IV. Patterns and Story Structure

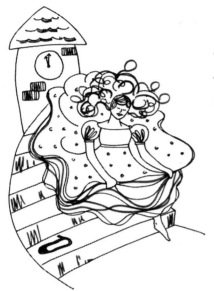

Translate the story of Cinderella from formal register and story structure into casual register and story structure.

V. Real-Life Applications

1. Translate interview questions into a future picture.
    Why are you applying to this school?
    Why should we hire you for this job?
    Why are you the best candidate for this position?
    Why *do* you want to work here?
    What would like us to know that we did not ask about?

2. Translate gratitude and courtesy into words.
    Write a thank you note to someone who has assisted or inspired you.
    ✋ Use a good pen and nice, unlined paper or a card.
    ✋ Review with your teacher and make revisions as needed before sending.

First line: In the upper right-hand corner, the date—spelled out (for example, October 20, 2014).
Next line: Dear (name of person you are thanking)—end the line with a comma.
Next lines: Thank you for (description and explanation).
Next lines: Mention something about the giver (I am very fortunate to know you).
Close with: "Thank you again," "Regards," or "Sincerely," with a comma at the end of the line.
Sign your name (first name only if you are acquainted with the individual).

3. In the space below, compose an email to a business requesting a refund for a product or service that did not meet your expectations.

VI. Sentence Structure in Formal Register

Sentence Frame

Reminds me that a sentence must have a capital letter at the beginning and a stop sign at the end. The effect of the sentence is expressed by the question mark (?) above the period or the exclamation point (!) above the period.

? . !

Bare-Bones Sentence

Teri danced.

A sentence must contain a subject and a predicate. The predicate can be an action predicate word.
Example: Teri danced.

Or the predicate can be a bound predicate.
Example: Teri is dancing.

The subject names a **person**, **place**, **thing**, or **idea**.

The action predicate expresses physical or mental action such as the following examples.

moved   kicked   thought   imagined

Predicate Expanders

The predicate can be expanded by expressing the how   when   where   why   of the action.

Example:

The waves pounded / relentlessly / against the small boat / as the fisherman struggled to reach shore .
                    (how)   (where)   (when)

Predicate Expanders:

How	=	degree	adverbs (-ly ending, like or as, with/without)
When	=	time	before, during, after, when, while, since
Where	=	position	prepositional phrases (to, from, against, behind)
Why	=	reason	because, to, so, for

Subject Describer

Words that describe physical characteristics, personality, numbers, and ownership.

Source: Project Read

Summarize in Casual Register

VII. Vocabulary

1. Learn Textbook and Test Vocabulary

The question on the test was:
Johnny has three green apples and seven red apples. Draw a table to compare the apples.

1. The Word, Term, or Concept	
2. Definition	3. In Your Words
textbook text technical term	
4. Mental Model	5. Connections
6. Home Language	

The vocabulary words the student learned were *chart* and *graph,* not *table.*

✋ Use the bold words and headings in the textbook to study.
Change bold text and headings into questions.
Answer with textbook words.

2. Learn Declarative and Procedural Words

Declarative: Word, term, or label
Procedural: Action, process, steps to complete the assignment

Declarative—What	Procedural—How
Essay	Write
Graphic organizer	Compare
Data	Formulate
	Analyze
	Contrast

What percentage of each type of information is needed to "master" these subjects?

	Declarative—What	Procedural—How
English		
Science		
Mathematics		
Geography		
History		

Hal Robertson, 2005

✋ Learn processes; use procedural self-talk and step sheets.

VII. Vocabulary

3. Create word walls in your classroom.
   Create electronic word walls.

Point Line Plane	Midpoint	Angle Bisector	Good Definition
Right Angle Acute Angle Obtuse Angle	Complementary Angles	Supplementary Angles	Vertical Angles
Linear Pair	Consecutive	Diagonal	Convex Polygon Concave Polygon
Equilateral Polygon Equiangular Polygon Regular Polygon	Right Triangle Acute Triangle Obtuse Triangle	Scalene Triangle Isosceles Triangle Equilateral Triangle	Trapezoid
Kite	Parallelogram	Rhombus	Rectangle
Square	Chord Diameter	Venn Diagram	Tangent

VIII. GAME DAYS!

Create and use games to build vocabulary and have FUN!

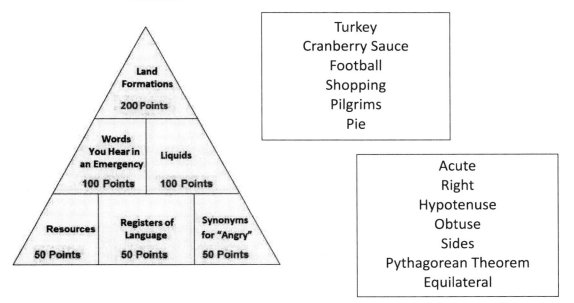

Turkey
Cranberry Sauce
Football
Shopping
Pilgrims
Pie

Acute
Right
Hypotenuse
Obtuse
Sides
Pythagorean Theorem
Equilateral

VIII. GAME DAYS!

Science	Social Studies	Math	Language Arts	Sports/Arts	General
100	100	100	100	100	100
200	200	200	200	200	200
300	300	300	300	300	300
400	400	400	400	400	400
500	500	500	500	500	500

ALBUQUERQUE SQUARES

TIC TAC TOE

Dow Jones X	share O	market value X
options O	bonds X	
bear market X		earnings O

IX. R Rules Raffiti

Kathleen Kuiper, the editor of *Merriam-Webster's Encyclopedia of Literature,* says:

"It is through the naming of objects, telling of stories, and singing of songs that we know ourselves and others. Whether trickster tales or nursery rhymes are the first thing we remember hearing, we have learned to live our lives by means of narrative—the stories our mothers told us, the books our brothers and sisters read to us (and the volumes we chose to read to them), and the holy books and textbooks that we read and memorized as children and still recall with perfect clarity. By these means we develop, however weakly or strongly, our moral natures, we discover who we are and who we are not, what we would give anything to be, and precisely what we would be willing to sacrifice to gain the prize. We need stories and songs to live."

> What is your favorite story?
> Share a funny story, an event, or a memory.

IX. Register

1. Register Review
2. Future and Current Pictures
3. SAFE—Standard American Formal English
4. Patterns and Story Structures
5. Real-Life Applications
6. Formal Sentence Structure
7. Vocabulary Builders
8. Game Day
9. Raffiti, Reflect, Resources

4.0	I understand the chapter and can teach the concepts I learned to others. What I learned is important and can be used in the following ways:	
3.0	I understand the chapter and do not have any questions about the concepts. What I learned is important because:	
2.0	I understand parts of this chapter. I still don't understand and have questions about:	
1.0	I still need help to understand the basic concepts of this chapter. Specifically about:	
I will apply what I learned in this chapter by:		

Rubric by K. Dixon

IX. Register Definitions, Symbols, Mental Models, Tools

Definitions

Declarative language: Word, term, or label. (What)

Predicate: One of the main parts of a sentence—subject is the other; verb.

Procedural: Action, process, steps to complete the assignment. (How)

Subject: Person, place, thing, idea; noun.

Symbols and Mental Models

Chapter 7 Relationships—Learning Objectives

What?	Why?	How?
I. Relationships	Define and discuss importance of relationships.	Discussion. Gather input on what students would like to learn on this topic.
II. Personal Relationships	Present activities and information that build relationships and social capital. Progress check on community resource project.	Activities that build resources for relationships: strengths, listening, relationship collage, sharing recipes, manners. Resources for teen dating.
III. Relationship Bank Account	Mental model for building relationships.	Use mental models to see different points of view and their relevance to relationships.
IV. Road Trip Relationships	Virtual travel to build skills and resources related to personal, interpersonal, and geographic relationships.	Organize a virtual trip; create an itinerary, budget, and expense report. Presentation on travel and process to class.
V. Learning Relationships	Increase awareness of relationships between school and work. Identify community resources and relationships.	Identify jobs, careers, and skills related to coursework. Identify relationships and resources that provide learning opportunities.
VI. School to Work Relationships	Identify relationships between necessary skills at work and school.	Identify and chart relationships between skills necessary to achieve at school and work.
VII. Student-Selected Topics		
VIII. Student-Selected Topics		
IX. Raffiti, Rubric, Resources	Clarify information, reflect, and define mental models.	Build knowledge, resources, and vocabulary.
Check items to be filed in your R Rules Personal Planner.		

Chapter 7—Relationships

I. Relationships are the connections, interactions, and patterns between people or things.

 **Rules – Relationships = Rebellion**
—Grant East

No significant learning occurs without a significant relationship.
—Dr. James Comer

Learning Relationships
What we learn is influenced by our relationships …
with the people we are learning from—
with the people we are learning for—
with what and why we are learning.

To get resources, results, and respect—
understand the rules, rigor, and *relationships*.

What *do* you want to learn about relationships?

II. Personal Relationships

Friends List five characteristics that are important for a friend to have.
1.
2.
3.
4.
5.

Friends List the five qualities that best describe you.
1.
2.
3.
4.
5.

Strength Quest
1. Every student in the class writes their name on a large, lined note card.
2. Students number the card with one number for each student in the group. (25 students, 1–25)
3. Pass cards around. Students identify one personal strength or talent of each student in the group and write it on that individual's card.
4. Cards are handed to teacher and reviewed. Students receive a participation grade.
5. Cards are returned to students and filed in personal planner.

Speed Talk
1. Students form two circles, one circle inside the other.
2. Students face each other.
3. When the timer begins, students share information with the person standing across from them for one minute.
4. One student talks, and the other listens.
5. Topics are called out by the facilitator.
6. After one minute, students move to the right or left as directed by the teacher.
7. Activity continues until facilitator calls time.

Develop your "elevator speech."

II. Personal Relationships

Create a photo collage of personal relationships for your personal planner. Cover one of the dividers in your planner with pictures of people that represent important relationships. Pictures might include family, friends, pets, or teams.

Update calendar weekly. Look at the dividers, reflect on relationships, note birthdays, make a note to talk with someone you haven't seen recently or to send a card, email, or schedule a visit. Schedule and honor as you would any important commitment or appointment.

Share a favorite recipe with your class. Discuss relevance of food to relationships. Present the recipe to the class. Include where the recipe originated, why it is your favorite, and any traditions associated with the recipe. Complete a plus delta evaluation of presentations.

Challenge yourself to select one staff member or teacher at your school who is not currently teaching any of your classes. At least three times each week, say hello to this person. Develop a relationship of mutual respect.

Manners are an internal resource. Develop and practice.
Use please, thank you, and excuse me. EXCUSE ME?!
Use names, and address people using a title of respect: "Mr. Smith" instead of "Hey, Joe."
Use adult voice; check your voice for volume and body language.
What are the hidden rules?

Card Check
How do each of the following influence relationships?

a. Expectations
b. Mental Models
c. Assumptions
d. Hidden Rules
e. Language
f. Experiences
g. Resources
h. Culture
i. Habits

What cards and rules did you bring from other relationships?

II. Personal Relationships

February is Teen Dating Violence Awareness Month.
Check out local and state websites as part of your community resource project.
Review a tool kit by teens at:
http://www.ped.state.nm.us/SchoolFamilySupport/dl09/2009%20NM%20TDV%20Toolkit%20(2).pdf

What does "respect" really mean?

The tool kit above shares this on respect: "Respect means a lot of different things. We have been taught to show respect to our elders, pay respect to others, and have self-respect. *Respect* is the number-one quality in a healthy relationship. **To show respect in a relationship means:**

- Making healthy decisions.
- Talking honestly and openly.
- Trusting each other.
- Valuing each other's independence.
- Building up each other's self-esteem.
- Supporting each other in going after goals and dreams.
- Encouraging each other to spend time with friends and family **and alone**.
- Having freedom to be yourself.
- Saying you're sorry when you make a mistake and learn from it."

Agreements
We agree to speak up if something is bothering us.
We agree to consider each other's feelings when talking to each other.
We agree to support each other when times are hard.
We agree to respect each other's privacy.
We agree to respect each other's space to be with other friends **and alone**.

How do you define respect?
What would you write in an agreement?
Do the guidelines above support every relationship? Family? Friends?

III. Relationship Bank Account

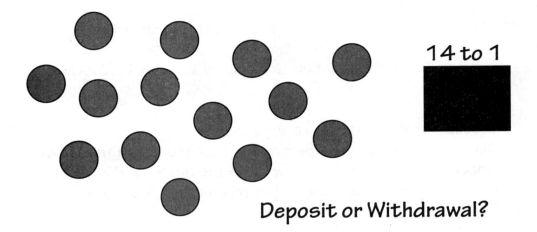

14 to 1

Deposit or Withdrawal?

Your parents haven't seen the prom dress you picked out, but they gave you the money to buy it.

You were invited to a birthday party, but you did not go.

Your mother served a special family recipe for dinner.

Your boyfriend/girlfriend told you, "Your house sure is different from mine."

Kate missed school, so you got her homework and took it to her.

You and a friend talked about another friend.

You took your grandmother to lunch at a fast food drive-in.

The teacher asked and told you in class: "Can you help this girl?"

The principal recognized you for an achievement during the assembly.

When you were shopping, a salesperson referred to you as "honey."

IV. Road Trip Relationships

Take a Road Trip

Working in teams, plan and take a virtual road trip.
Travel must be to a destination you have not previously visited.
Develop an itinerary for your trip that includes times, activities, tours, and costs.
Research attractions and activities such as: museums, entertainment, and historic sites.
Create an information file to use as a reference while you travel—include resources
   such as websites, contacts, and phone and confirmation numbers.
Create and use a written budget.
Show all expenses, and turn in an expenditure report.
Develop a presentation for class. Include photos and information about your trip.
Additional details will be provided by your instructor.

Support Systems

Who or what will provide support if you need assistance while you are traveling?
What navigation systems do you use when traveling?
If your GPS or electronics were disabled, how would you navigate in a new location?
How do you locate north, south, east, and west?
What patterns are available and could be used to assist your navigation?
Where will you travel in relationship to where you currently live?

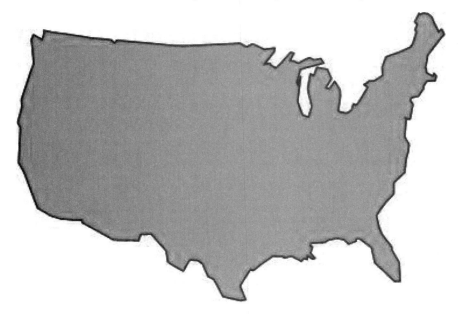

V. Learning Relationships

School to Work

WHAT	WHY	HOW
Algebra	Solving for the unknown through functions.	
Biology	Identifying living systems and relationships within.	
Chemistry	Bonding.	
Earth Science	Identifying and predicting physical phenomena.	
Geometry	Using logic to order and assign values to forms and space.	
Language Arts	Using structure and language to communicate.	
Math	Assigning value and order to the universe.	
Physics	Using matter and energy through math applications.	
Social Studies	Identifying patterns of people and governments over time.	

How are the subjects above related to real life?
List jobs and careers these subjects are related to.

How does what you are learning relate to your future picture?
To your current picture?
The ability to see relationships can help you get through a difficult job or class
 you don't particularly like.
Look to your "end in mind" to find and use "learning relationships" and reach goals.

Community

List places or people in your community that provide learning relationships and
 resources such as: technology, tutoring, and language classes. Include them in
 your community resource project.

VI. School to Work Relationships

What are your employable skills?
Employers evaluate performance to determine promotions and salary.
Use the chart below to show the relationship between skills for work and school.

Evaluation Criteria	Leader/Manager	Employee	Termination
Attendance			
Punctual			
Team Member			
Independent Worker			
Behavior			
Dress			
Approach			
Communication			
Learner			
Language			
Contributes			
Math and Technology			
Follows Directions			
Open to New Ideas			
Completes Jobs			
Manages Resources			
Safety			
Prepared			
Time Management			

VII.

VIII.

IX. R Rules Raffiti

Check your cards.
What five relationships are most important to you?
Why?

IX. Relationships

1. Relationships
2. Personal Relationships
3. Relationship Bank Account
4. Virtual Road Trip
5. Learning Relationships
6. School to Work Relationships
7. Topic Selected by Students
8. Raffiti, Reflect, Reference

4.0	I understand the chapter and can teach the concepts I learned to others. What I learned is important and can be used in the following ways:
3.0	I understand the chapter and do not have any questions about the concepts. What I learned is important because:
2.0	I understand parts of this chapter. I still don't understand and have questions about:
1.0	I still need help to understand the basic concepts of this chapter. Specifically about:

I will demonstrate information learned in this chapter by:

Rubric by K. Dixon

IX. Relationships Definitions, Symbols, Mental Models, Tools

Definitions

Relationships: The connections, interactions, or patterns between people or things. Relationships are as unique as the individuals, times, and places in which they occur. Relationships often have agreed-upon behaviors, rules, and roles.

Symbols and Mental Models

Chapter 8 Review—Learning Objectives

What?	Why?	How?
I. Review: To View Again	21st century skills include the ability to problem solve and use critical and creative thinking.	Use creative and critical thinking to answer questions and solve puzzles.
II. Review Paradigms	Increase awareness of mental models, attitudes, and patterns of thinking.	Learn about paradigms, paradigm shifts, and their relevance to achievement and well-being.
III. Think Different	Review mental models to avoid limited thinking. Humor is a coping and resilience strategy.	Discussion to increase awareness and use of humor as a resilience strategy. Define and explore emotional comfort zone.
IV. Review for Resilience	Resilience strategies are an important resource.	Learn and use strategies and resources for resilience. Discuss emotional memory bank.
V. Review for Resources	Identify resources and mental models for self-assessment.	Use mental models to increase awareness and build resources.
VI. Think Different Role Models	Role models are an emotional resource that can encourage and inspire.	View slide presentation, identify role models, and present personal role models.
VII. Think Different	Increase awareness of advertising campaigns and literature.	Read and discuss text.
VIII. Free Fall	Responses to develop resources and increase self-awareness.	Respond to survey and use the information to plan and develop resources.
IX. Think Different in Story	Story about different paradigms.	Read and discuss the story.
X. Think Zebra	Identify personal role models.	Identify 10 people—from the past or present—you would invite to dinner.
XI. Raffiti, Rubric, Definitions	Clarify information, reflect, and define mental models.	Build knowledge, resources, and vocabulary.
Check items to be filed in your R Rules Personal Planner.		

Chapter 8—Review

1. To view again
   To see in new ways

1. Draw one straight line through all nine dots.

2. Connect all nine dots with only four lines.

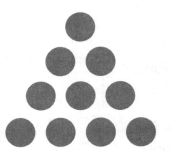

3. Flip the triangle by moving only three dots.

4. Cut a cupcake into eight equal pieces with only three cuts of the knife.

5. Follow directions using a blank sheet of paper.

6. What is the only number that is spelled in alphabetical order?

The Eagle Chick

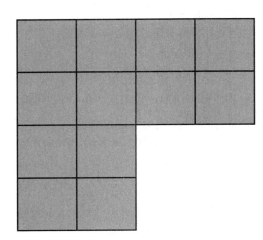

7. Subdivide the farmer's land into four pieces of equal size and shape for distribution to his four children.

II. Review Paradigms

Paradigm: How we view the world, the patterns, attitude and beliefs—
 our mental model or assumption—of how things are or should be.
Paradigm Shift: A shift or change in thinking or attitude due to new learning
 or understanding.   https://www.youtube.com/watch?v=SiNEIKx64f0

Is your glass half full or half empty?

 Fish see water last.

We all have the same option—24 hours.

Review to:
 Listen to your voice. Is your glass half full or half empty?
 Understand your habits.
 Like fish seeing water—you may require new views.
 Increase awareness about what is important to you.
 See new options and possibilities, and avoid "limiting thinking."
 Develop and use mental models about "thinking different."

The eagle chick lived his entire life using a limiting paradigm.
 How do you see yourself?
 What are your paradigms?

Thomas Edison said, "If we did all of the things we are capable of doing, we would literally astound ourselves." Go ahead ... *amaze and astound!* Just do it!

III. Think Different

Comedians are masters at "thinking different" and generating new points of view.

As a comedian was entering the hospital, a reporter asked how long his stay would be. He replied, "About two weeks if things go well; about two hours if they don't."

> "My parents always told me, 'Stay away from the cellar door!'
> But one day I had to see what was on the other side.
> When I opened it I saw wonderful things I'd never seen before ...
> Like trees, and grass, and the sun."   —Emo Philips, comic

Humor is a strategy for resilience. When things are tough, or when you are out of your comfort zone, finding something that is funny in the situation can get you through. The trick is to understand the "hidden rules" of the environment or situation. Laughing or humor during a test, business meeting, or serious conversation can reduce stress. It can also break hidden rules and generate a new round of stress.

♻ **Emotional Comfort Zone:** Term for situations and environments that are familiar, where we feel emotionally safe or in control. Examples: activities and places where we understand the rules and expectations and feel safe to contribute and achieve.

Reflect on a time you were out of your emotional comfort zone.
What strategies or resources did you use?
Create and use an "R Rules resource zone."

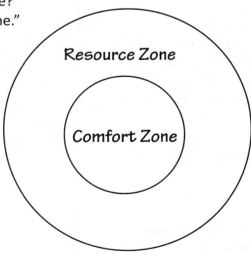

IV. Review for Resilience

> **Resilience:** The ability to spring back, recover, or rebound from exposure to extreme stress, unhealthy situations, or adverse experiences (resiliency).

Review Your Resilience Resources

1. Use affirmations. See examples on the following page; write your own.

2. Review your self-talk. Avoid negative self-talk. Flip if from "I can't" to "I can."

3. Develop the adult voice. Children must often act as adults. A child here is defined as anyone under the age of 18. Children who act as adults generally have two voices: the parent voice and the child voice. Develop and use the adult voice.

4. Stop negative self-talk using parent and adult voice. Say in the parent voice, "Stop!" then redirect and encourage using the adult voice. Say in the adult voice: "If I could get my driver's license, I can pass this test." Then ...

5. Use procedural self-talk to start and complete the work: "First I will ... , then I will ... "

6. To disengage emotions ... *look up.*

7. Consider your emotional memory bank. The mind stores experiences and the emotions attached to them in an "emotional memory bank." In a given situation, the mind accesses emotions of a past event. Even though the current event is totally different, the individual connects the current event to a past event or experience and reacts accordingly. Disengage your emotions to focus and respond to the actual, current situation or event.

IV. Review for Resilience

1. Eliminate Negative Self-Talk
Use Affirmations

> I can ...
> I will ...
> I increase my knowledge every day.
> I am a champion.
> I have resources to ...
> I use my unique strengths and talents to ...
> What I imagine, I can do.
> I am learning (what) from this (experience).
> All things are working together for my good.
> I speak confidently and clearly.
> I have a clear vision and am making progress toward my goals.
> If I could do (that), then I can do (this).
> I am growing stronger every day.
> I am respectful of others, and I live in peace.
> As I change the way I think, I change the way my life goes.
> When I finish this I am going to celebrate by ...
> I am a good person.
> My life is an adventure.
> I have courage to try new things.
> My present thoughts shape my future.

2. Use Quotations and Songs That Inspire

Nelson Mandela	"The greatest glory in living lies not in never falling, but in rising every time we fall."
Bishop Macklin	"I see my tomorrow and I see my today. I look even better in my tomorrow than I do in my today."
W Mitchell	"It's not what happens to you, it is what you do about it."
Steve Maraboli	"When times are tough, dare to be tougher."
Robert Collier	"Visualize this thing you want. See it, feel it, believe in it. Make a mental blueprint and begin to build."

Create a playlist of songs that represent who you are;
use it to inspire and motivate.

V. Review for Resources

REVIEW the way you see yourself and the way others see you.
- Look at yourself in the MIRROR then through the WINDOW.
- Use this mental model to increase self-awareness.
- Look in the MIRROR to see and learn about yourself.
- Look through the WINDOW to understand how others see you.
- Use the information to identify and build resources.
- Look at current and future pictures and use to guide decisions and plan.

FAIL FORWARD
- We have all experienced results that were not what we expected or wanted.
- Use the experience as an opportunity to learn, plan, and change behaviors or habits in order to move forward toward your goals.

TIME
- Develop habits that reduce stress and increase your ability to plan and manage time.
- Habits are behaviors that are repeated and automatic.
- Example: Get in the habit of always storing your keys and phone in the same place.

REVIEW and REFLECT
- Go from the FIELD to the BLEACHERS.
- Use this mental model to take time out, leave the game to reflect, look at patterns, and review and revise your game plan.

SCHEDULE TIME
- Schedule one day each week to review and update your calendar and plan for the week.
- Look at your future picture.
- Look at the words you live by—respect, family, strength, and health.
- Look at your goals.
- Look at assignments, important events, and commitments for the upcoming week.
- Write things that *must or need* to be done—day and times—on your calendar.
    - Examples: birthdays, events, a dance, practice, game times, an English assignment.
- Then write things you would like or hope to do.
    - Examples: shop, watch a video, visit a friend.
- Schedule time and complete the *must* items first. When they are completed, if you have time, start on the "wants and hopes" list.

UNDERSTAND and MANAGE TIME
- How much can you get done in one minute?
- Watch the clock.
- *Listen* to someone talk for three minutes.

Create a mental model of one of the items above and display in your classroom.

V. Review for Resources

TIME

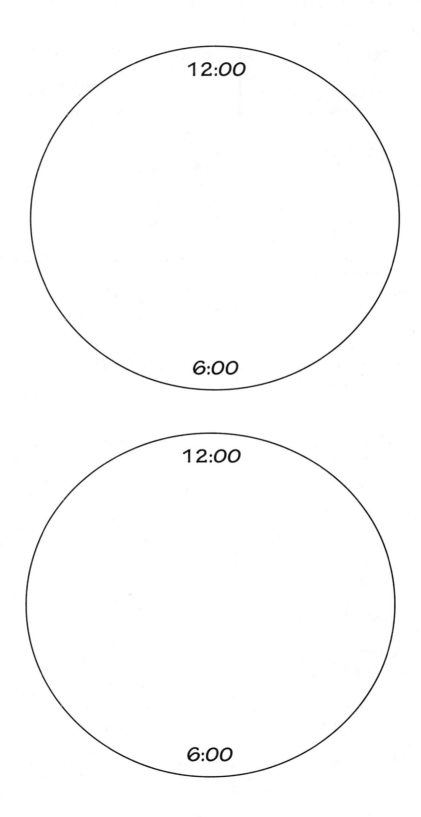

V. Review for Resources

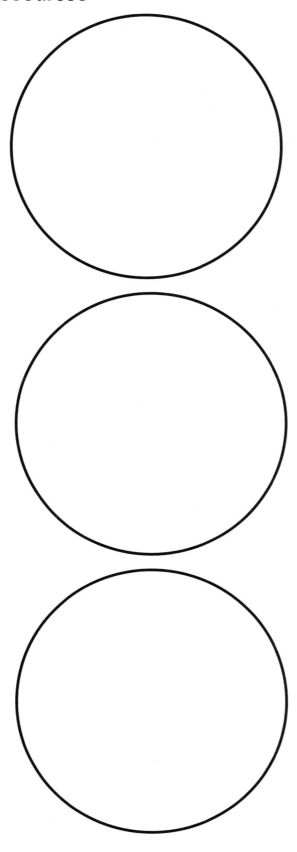

VI. Think Different Role Models

"Think Different" was an advertising slogan used by Apple Computer, Inc.

Apple Computer did not accept the paradigm that computers were not for home use.

Christopher Columbus did not accept the paradigm that the world was flat.

Nelson Mandela did not accept continued violence and revenge; he thought different and formed the Truth and Reconciliation Commission.

Leaders, dreamers, and pioneers have challenged paradigms all throughout history.

1. *View the "Think Different" slide presentation.*
   All of the individuals are recognized for their accomplishments and contributions.
   Several faced a language barrier.
   Some had learning disabilities.
   Some came from poverty, some from wealth.
   Some were immigrants.
   Each overcame challenges.
   Any of them could serve as a role model.
   Each discovered a talent and developed it.
   All had the courage to think different ...
   The ability to see themselves as they might be ...
   The resources to dream of what could be ...
   And the courage to say, "I will be."

2. *Journal about the difference you would like to make.*
   Your mind is a tool to invent and discover.
   Your mind is a weapon to fight fear and injustice.
   Your mind is a resource to create the world we all want to live in.

3. *Identify and develop a presentation.*
   Present on two individuals you admire for their accomplishments and courage.
   Follow instructions, process, and rubric as directed by your instructor.

VII. Think Different

>Here's to the crazy ones.
>The misfits.
>The rebels.
>The round pegs in square holes.
>The ones who see things differently.
>They are not fond of rules ...
>because they change things.
>They invent.
>They imagine.
>They heal.
>They explore.
>They create.
>They inspire.
>While some call them crazy,
>others see genius.
>Because the people who are crazy enough
>to think they can change the world ...
>are the ones who do.
>
>Adapted from the Apple Computer "Think Different"
>Campaign, Apple Computer, Inc., 1992.

"Be the change that you wish to see in the world."
—Mahatma Gandhi

"All men dream: but not equally.
Those who dream by night
in the dusty recesses of their mind
wake in the morning to find that it was vanity;
but the dreamers of the day are dangerous men,
for they may act their dreams with open eyes,
to make it possible."
—T. E. Lawrence

What *do* you dream?

VIII. Free Fall

You will not be asked to share your responses. You will use them to see patterns and identify resources. After you have written your responses, discussion will include information on each item and how it can be used to increase resources and support current and future pictures. File a copy in your planner.

1. One thing that makes you **furious**. _____

2. Something you think is **funny**. _____

3. One thing you **fear**. _____

4. Who could/should you **forgive**. _____

5. One thing you do that is **fabulous!** _____

6. Three qualities of a **friend**. _____

7. What do you have **faith in?** _____

8. If you could **fix** anything, what would it be? _____

9. What comes to mind when you think of **freedom?** _____

10. What would you try if you knew you could not **fail?** _____

11. What would you do if it was **free?** _____

12. What is your greatest hope for the **future?** _____

"Too often we are scared.
Scared of what we might not be able to do.
Scared of what people might think if we tried.
We let our fears stand in the way of our hopes."

Words in this Nike ad featuring Barry Sanders are an inspiration to me. Read the entire ad at: http://media-cache-ec0.pinimg.com/736x/88/53/bc/8853bc19c9d84cdd56860749b98c4496.jpg

IX. Think Different in Story

Think Rather of Zebra
by Jay Stailey and Ruby Payne

A student had studied for a long time and felt he was finally ready to leave his teacher.

"You are not ready," the teacher told him with a gentle smile.

"Why not?" asked the student, almost indignantly.

"You have not yet learned the meaning of story," replied the teacher.

The student looked so disappointed that his teacher added quietly, "Stories can teach us a new way of seeing things, of thinking about them, and of responding."

Because he could see that his student still did not understand, the wise teacher reached out to help once again. "When you hear hoofbeats, what do you think of?" he questioned in a soft voice.

"Why, a horse, certainly!" answered the student with confidence.

"That is because you have become conditioned, and in that conditioning you have fallen asleep," the patient teacher pointed out. "When you hear hoofbeats—think rather of zebra."

In the eye of the student a glimmer of understanding shone. Turning to the teacher, he said, "Tell me a story."

X. Think Zebra

If you could invite 10 people to dinner—10 individuals who are currently living—or who lived in the past—to dinner and an evening of conversation ... who would you invite?

XI. R Rules Raffiti

 THINK

From this hour I ordain myself
loos'd of limits and imaginary lines.
                –Walt Whitman

XI. Review

1. Critical and Creative Thinking
2. Paradigms
3. Resilience Strategies
4. Role Models
5. "Think Different" Texts
6. Free Fall
7. Story: Think Zebra
8. Raffiti, Reflect, Reference

4.0	I understand the chapter and can teach the concepts I learned to others. What I learned is important and can be used in the following ways:	
3.0	I understand the chapter and do not have any questions about the concepts. What I learned is important because:	
2.0	I understand parts of this chapter. I still don't understand and have questions about:	
1.0	I still need help to understand the basic concepts of this chapter. Specifically about:	

My plan to use information I learned in this chapter is:

Rubric by K. Dixon

XI. Review Definitions, Symbols, Mental Models, Tools

Definitions

Creative thinking: Thinking that involves creating something new or original.

Critical thinking: Thinking that involves applying reasoning and logic.

Emotional comfort zone: Term for situations and environments that are familiar and where we feel emotionally safe or in control. Places and activities where we understand the rules and expectations and feel safe to contribute and achieve.

Emotional memory bank: Term for part of the mind where experiences and the emotions attached to them are stored.

Habits: Patterns of behaviors that are repeated and almost become involuntary.

Paradigm: How we view the world, the patterns, attitudes, and beliefs—our mental model or assumption—of how things are or should be.

Paradigm shift: Shift or change in thinking or attitude due to new learning or understanding.

Resilience: Ability to spring back, recover, or rebound from exposure to extreme stress, unhealthy situations, or adverse experiences.

Symbols and Mental Models

Think Zebra — Think in new ways and see new and different options

Think — Think out of the box; avoid limited or "boxed in" thinking

Chapter 9 Response—Learning Objectives

What?	Why?	How?
I. Champions Circle of Control	Mental models to identify factors individuals can and cannot control.	Mental models for responses and choice based on resources.
II. Choice	Mental models for choice to build resources for responding in various situations.	Discuss and use mental models to guide personal choices.
III. Patterns for Response	Present mental models that can be used to develop internal resources.	Use mental models—graphics and scenarios—to develop resources and skills for responding.
IV. I Tell Myself a Story	Use mental models to gather, sort, and apply information.	Use mental models and tools to determine what is important and what is not and manage responses.
V. Resources	Identify resources that increase stability, reduce stress, and assist in responding.	Identify and develop internal and external resources for responding in various situations.
VI. Predict and Plan	Direct instruction on relevance of identifying patterns and planning.	Review text, video, and actual court cases. Discuss cause and effect, choices, and consequences to identify and develop resources.
VII. Emotional Blackmail	Teach the what, why, how, when, and where strategy as a tool for responding to emotional blackmail.	Use what, why, how, when, and where strategy as a tool for sorting information and responding.
VIII. Raffiti, Rubric, Definitions	Clarify information, reflect, and define mental models.	Build knowledge, resources, and vocabulary.
Check items to be filed in your R Rules Personal Planner.		

Chapter 9—Response

I. Circle of Control

> Champions are not made in the ring,
> they are just recognized there. –Unknown

Mahatma Gandhi's daughter tells the story of her father arriving in South Africa and being thrown off of the train because of the color of his skin. He was so humiliated that he spent the rest of the night wondering what he would do to get justice for such an injustice.

She shares that his first response was anger—an eye for an eye. His second was to go back to India where he was respected and accepted. Then he considered a third response—nonviolence. This choice remained Gandhi's way for his entire life. He spent 22 years in South Africa making a difference there and inspiring other leaders all over the world.
—Arun Ghandi, *Reflections on Working Toward Peace*

Victor Frankl wrote in his book *Man's Search for Meaning* about men in the German concentration camps walking through the huts, caring for others, even giving away their last pieces of bread. He goes on to say that though they were few in number, these men proved that every freedom could be taken from a man but one. He calls this "the last of human freedoms," which is the right in any situation "to choose one's own way."

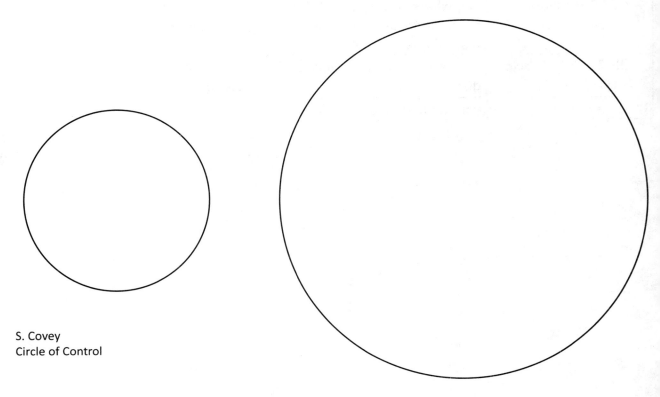

S. Covey
Circle of Control

II. Choice

You can't control the cards you were dealt.
You can *control* and *choose* how you play them.

VOICE   SELF-TALK
ATTITUDE   RESPONSE TIME
EMOTION   DISTANCE
HUMOR   GRAVITY

When President Kennedy was asked by a reporter how he became a war hero, he replied, "It was involuntary. They sank my boat."

W Mitchell—
"It is not what happens to you.
It's what you *do* about it that matters."

http://www.wmitchell.com/video.html

III. Patterns for Response

1.

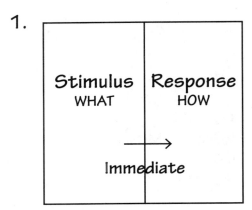

2.

| Stimulus
WHAT | WHY
⟶
Time
Resources
Values
Future Picture | Response
HOW |

 Resources are relevant to responses.
Proactive: Planning for opportunities and challenges.
Reactive: Responding or reacting as events occur.

Check it:
You just won three tickets to a concert that will be held in your city next month.
On the way home from school, your car quit running.
Your teacher is very demanding. He mentioned your attitude in class today.
You have three new text messages.
Your friend wants to borrow money.
Your grandma needed help, and you were late for school.
You got a call to come to an interview for a job tomorrow.
You write one …

IV. I Tell Myself a Story

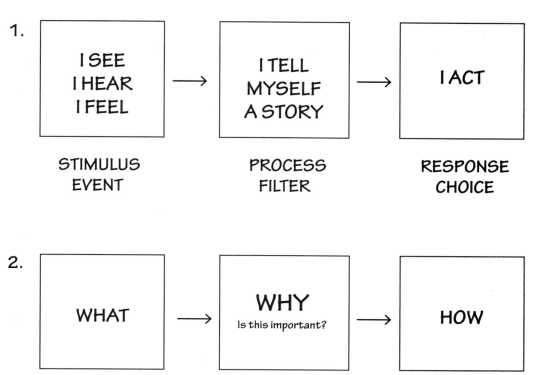

ASK
How much *time* do I have before I have to respond?
Do I *have* to respond?
Do I *need* to respond?

Disengage Emotions

V. Resources

Personal and Community
  Develop resources that increase stability and reduce stress.
  Identify personal, institutional, and community resources; learn how to access and use them.
  Review and understand policies.
  More resources = more choices.

End in Mind
  Review your current and future pictures.
  Determine what is important to you, and use it to help make decisions.
  Understand and use hidden rules and goals of the environment you are in.
  Develop and use an adult voice when responding.
  Use patterns to predict and plan how you want to respond.
  Develop plans that can reduce stress, maintain safety, and build mutual respect.

Check Emotional Resources
  Anger is related to fear. Understand what you are afraid of, and determine if the fear is justified.
  Find humor in the situation.
  Understand that unspoken responses are as important as spoken responses.
  Respond using behaviors that are not destructive to you or others.
  Look for patterns to predict, and develop responses in order to control what you can.
  Understand your emotional memory bank, and develop response resources.
  Build a strong "emotional resource zone."

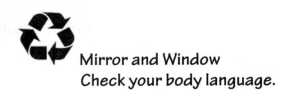

Mirror and Window
Check your body language.

VI. Predict and Plan

When you can see a pattern ... you can predict.

When you can predict ... you can identify cause and effect.

When you can identify cause and effect ... you can identify outcomes.

When you can identify outcomes ...

        Choices and Consequences
        Teen Pranks
        The Stop Sign Case

Cards of Fate
Scenarios

VII. Emotional Blackmail

Everybody says ...
   He or she said ...
     They said ...

Stay in the adult voice. Control body language and emotions.

Accept that the person truly believes what he or she is telling you. (It is their reality.)

Get specifics and facts by using: *when, where, how, which ones.*

Ask, "When specifically did this happen?" or "Where specifically did this happen?"

Avoid nonspecifics (everybody, she, he, or they). Nonspecifics make it impossible to clarify or understand the situation.

Talk about the problem or the situation—not the person or people.

Avoid blaming.

 What, why, how, when, where

VIII. R Rules Raffiti

VIII. Response

1. Circle of Control
2. Choices
3. Mental Models
4. I Tell Myself a Story
5. Resources
6. Plan and Predict
7. Emotional Blackmail
8. Raffiti, Reflect, Resources

4.0	I understand the chapter and can teach the concepts I learned to others. What I learned is important and can be used in the following ways:	
3.0	I understand the chapter and do not have any questions about the concepts. What I learned is important because:	
2.0	I understand parts of this chapter. I still don't understand and have questions about:	
1.0	I still need help to understand the basic concepts of this chapter. Specifically about:	

I will respond to what I learned in this chapter by:

Rubric by K. Dixon

VIII. Response Definitions, Symbols, Mental Models, Tools

Definitions

Proactive: Acting in advance to plan for opportunities and challenges.

Reactive: Responding or reacting as events occur.

Symbols and Mental Models

Reframe It

Chapter 10 Reframe—Learning Objectives

What?	Why?	How?
I. Benny Barnes	Present a story as a mental model, and discuss reframing a future picture.	Read and discuss the story of Benny Barnes.
II. Mental Models	Mental models reframe and compress learning time.	Use mental models to reframe.
III. Organizers and Charts	Understand various options to reframe, analyze, and display information.	Create charts and use time management tools and graphic organizers.
IV. Reframe at School and Work	Various learning styles require different methods to sort, gather, and recall information.	Test questions, partnering study activity, summarizing, and locating information.
V. Reframe Reading	Skills to locate information in nonfiction reading materials.	Use strategies for reading materials at school and work.
VI. Question Making	Knowing how to frame and ask questions is a resource for learning, relationships, and self-advocacy.	Discuss and learn about reframing questions, identifying qualifiers, and using different voices.
VII. Reframe Learning Styles	Increase understanding of personal styles and use to develop resources for achievement.	Assess personal learning styles and develop resources based on various teaching styles.
VIII. Reframe Response	To provide direct instruction on reframing strategies.	Use reframing strategies: 1. "If you choose" 2. The four-step process 3. Reflection steps
IX. Raffiti, Rubric, Definition	Clarify information, reflect, and define mental models.	Build knowledge, resources, and vocabulary.
Check items to be filed in your R Rules Personal Planner.		

Chapter 10—Reframe

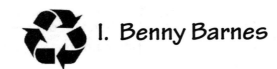 **I. Benny Barnes**

Reframe to:
offer a different perspective or option,
to look at, present, or see in a different way.

You cannot shake hands with a clenched fist.
—Indira Gandhi

 Every day in America, large numbers of students drop out of school.

WHY?

Reframe: Every single school day, 180 school buses drive out of America's school yards filled with students who will not return.

—Franklin Schargel, *Dropout Prevention Tools*

II. Mental Models
Benny Barnes

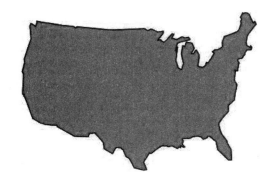

Stand in front of my desk.
I need the book that is sitting in Florida.

How many different types of shoes will you wear in your future picture?

Reframes for Math

+ Good Guy   + Comes to Town   + Good
− Bad Guy   − Leaves Town   − Bad
     +   +   +

The Journey of Al and Gebra to the Land of Algebra
— Bethanie Tucker

II. Mental Models
The Story of Coach 'Stump' Barnes

When I was in high school, I had a classmate named Benny Barnes. Benny was a couple of years older than I was. He was a senior when I was a sophomore. The reason I knew Benny was the same reason everybody knew Benny. He was a great athlete. He played on the football team and ran track, but he *was* the basketball team. In his junior year, Benny had been named second team all state. He was such a natural. Folks said he must have been born with a basketball in his hand. He was about six feet tall, which was pretty tall back then, and slim built. He was probably the closest thing to a Michael Jordan this city has ever seen.

Benny Barnes was not only great on the basketball court, he also was pretty good in the classroom. His mother was a smart lady but had never finished high school. She wanted nothing more than for Benny to get an education so he could take care of himself. Don't get me wrong, she was proud of what Benny could do on the football field and the basketball court, but her main concern was what he did in the classroom.

By the time Benny had finished his junior year, a few of the colleges were beginning to send scouts to watch him play. I remember when a couple of scouts from the big universities stood out in the crowd. Everybody knew they had come to watch Benny, and most folks hoped Benny would choose to go to one of the smaller schools. The truth of the matter was, it was Benny's mama who would do the choosing when the time came.

Obviously, something must have happened, or everybody would know who Benny Barnes was, and I wouldn't have to be telling you this story. One afternoon after practice, Benny was on his way home with his books and his basketball. During the season, Benny always had a ball in his hand. He was dribbling the ball and looking straight ahead. In order to get over to the Tree streets where he lived, he had to cross the railroad tracks. Since he was working on his dribbling, he usually walked all the way down to the crossing, though it was a little farther to get home that way. Some of the other kids had decided to cross over, and a few always walked down the track.

On this particular afternoon, there were two boys walking down the tracks parallel to Benny and headed in the same direction. I suppose he saw them but really didn't pay any attention until he heard the train whistle blow. At first he thought the boys were playing chicken. He used to do that himself before his mama caught him and took the belt to his rear end. Finally, he realized that the boy on the track wanted to get off; he just couldn't. Benny dropped his books and ball and sprinted toward the railroad tracks. Sure enough, the boy had somehow caught his shoe in one of the rails and couldn't move. The train was getting louder and louder, and eventually the sound of the train engine and the metal screeching of the brakes added to the boys' shouts and made the whole scene an incredible jumble of noise and fear.

II. Mental Models
The Story of Coach 'Stump' Barnes

Benny tugged and tugged on the boy's foot and at the last second managed to free it from the rail. The two of them fell to the side of the track and the boy, though frightened to death, was unhurt. When Benny tried to get up, he had a funny feeling in his left leg. He looked down and saw that it was worse than a funny feeling. His leg was missing from the knee down.

By that time the train had stopped and people were running from every direction. Eventually Doc Johnson arrived, and Benny went to the hospital. I think Benny's mama was hospitalized for a while, too. Some folks said that Benny's mama suffered more at the loss of that leg than Benny did. He got better, and the doctors fixed him up with a wooden leg. At first it was just a wooden peg, like the pirates had, but eventually someone donated some money and sent him to a hospital where he could get fitted with a leg that looked more real. But even that leg with the hand-carved foot couldn't hide Benny's limp. It couldn't get him back on the basketball court either. Worse than that to Benny's mother, Benny never showed up in the classroom again.

Over time, Benny left the neighborhood, and stories came back about drinking and drugs and trouble with the law. It always sounded worse than it really was, and no one ever talked bad about Benny himself. When Benny's mama left the neighborhood a couple of years after the accident, the only time Benny's name was ever mentioned was when an up-and-coming ballplayer did something exciting. Then folks would say he was a regular Benny Barnes.

About four years ago Mr. Woodson, down at the barbershop, got a letter from his cousin in St. Louis. In the letter there was a news clipping about the Missouri state championship high school basketball team. The article talked about how the team had been in the state finals three of the last five years and had won twice. The coach, when asked about the team's success, said, "If you want something badly enough, and are willing to work for it, you can accomplish lots more than a state championship."

The story also had a picture and caption: "Coach 'Stump' Barnes with State Championship Squad." There was a short paragraph in the story about the coach. It seemed Coach Barnes had lost part of a leg in an accident that ended his playing career, but had gone to school to become a teacher and later returned to his favorite pastime—basketball.

–from *Think Rather of Zebra: Dealing with Aspects of Poverty Through Story* by Jay Stailey and Ruby Payne

III. Organizers and Charts

1. Use the boxes below to sketch a book report or notes.
   Use to "chunk" or start a story: beginning, middle, and end.

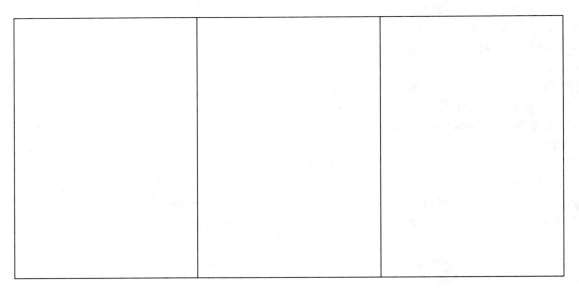

2. See similarities and differences.
   Compare two jobs that interest you, or compare work and school.

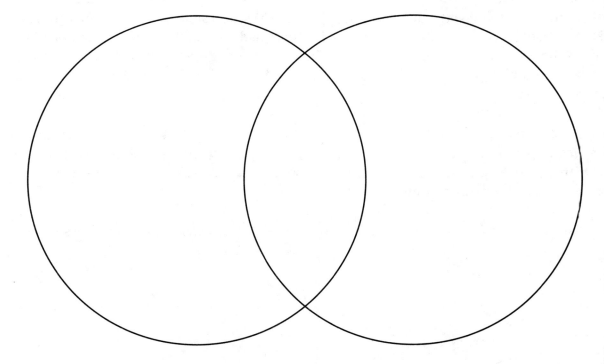

III. Organizers and Charts

3. Compare phone plans, colleges, or vehicles.

	Item 1	Item 2	Item 3	
Factor 1				Similar and Different
Factor 2				Similar and Different
Factor 3				Similar and Different

Adapted from Diane Paynter.

4. Create charts and graphs.
    Use sticky dots or sticky notes to chart answers to survey questions.
    Have fun!
    Chart your favorite colors, birthdates, types of cars, or ...

Health Science	Architecture Construction	Agriculture Natural Resources	Manufacturing	Hospitality Tourism

Chapter 10—Reframe 211

III. Organizers and Charts

5. Manage Time

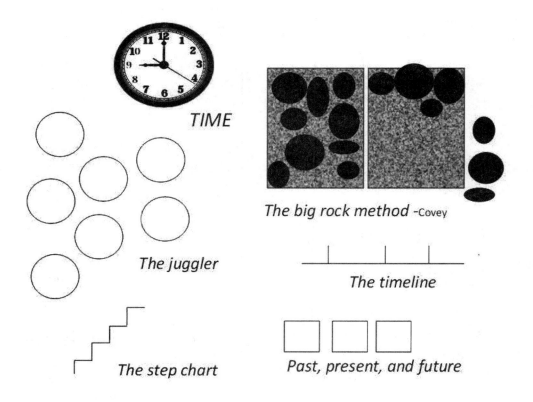

CHART IT!
21 days to change a habit!

Reframes to change a habit:

IV. Reframe at School and Work

A. Answer the phone and take a message for your boss. Listen ...

B. Questions from **Bold** Type
    1. Make questions out of the **bold text** your textbook.
    2. Answer the questions and use them to study.

C. Apples and Oranges
    1. Work with a partner.
    2. One person tells everything he/she knows about an apple.
    3. The other tells everything he/she knows about an orange.
    4. Either person shares anything else they can think of about an apple or orange.
    5. Compare how apples and oranges are alike and different.
    6. Use this to review or study for a test in any course.   –Jim Littlejohn

D. Summarize, Compare, and Contrast Information
    Day One
    1. With your class—view a presentation (YouTube, video, podcast).
    2. You may take notes individually during the presentation.
    3. After the presentation, as a group, record 5–7 key points of the presentation.
    4. Chart and post in the classroom.
    5. Other sections of the class will follow the same process.
    Day Two
    1. Review key points identified by other classes.
    2. Compare your own to the other classes'.
    3. Watch the video again.
    4. Discuss and revise key points as needed.
    5. Grade is given to team, not individuals.

    GEAR UP, Farmington Municipal Schools, New Mexico.

IV. Reframe at School and Work

E. Sketch
1. Photosynthesis
2. Carburetor
3. Onomatopoeia
4. A timeline
5. An event or process

F. Create and use your own mental models.

V. Reframe Reading

A Reading Strategy

1. Box in and read the title.
2. Trace and number the paragraphs.
3. Stop and think at the end of each paragraph to identify a key point.
4. Circle the key word or write the key point in the margin.
5. Read and label the key words in the questions.
6. Prove your answer. Locate the paragraph where the answer is found.
7. Mark or write your answer.

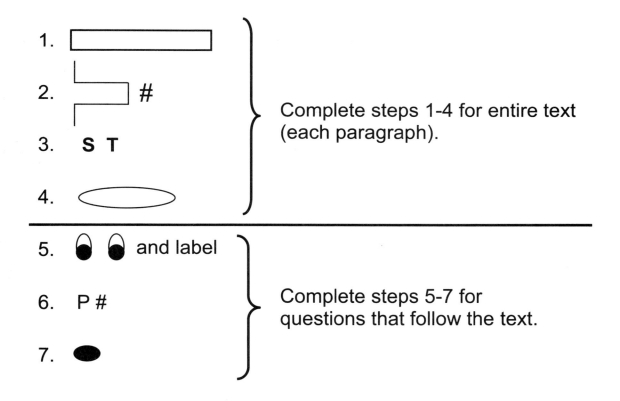

Source: Kim D. Ellis, *Putting the Pieces Together.*

VI. Question Making—Multiple Choice

Question:

Answers:

a.

b.

c.

d.

Three Rules:

1. One wrong answer must be funny.

2. Only one answer can be right.

3. Answer may not be "all of the above" or "none of the above."

VI. Question Making

1. KNOWLEDGE: Recall, recognize, demonstrate	2. COMPREHENSION: Understanding
Recalling: listing, defining, stating, describing, example **Recognizing:** choosing, selecting, picking, identifying **Demonstrating:** showing or doing What information is given? What are you being asked to find? When did the event take place? Point to the … List or sketch the … Name the … Where did …? Who was/were …? What events led to _____?	**Integrating:** explain, parts, how, effect, relationships **Symbolizing:** representing, charting, using models, using graphic organizers What are you being asked to find? What is an example of … What does this mean in your own words? What would happen to you if …? Would you have done the same thing as …? What other ways could ____ be interpreted? What information supports your view? What was the message of this story? Can you use a graphic organizer to explain?
3. APPLICATION: Use learning in new situations Combination of comprehension and analysis What would happen to you if …? Can you see a pattern or relationship? Would you have done the same thing as …? What occurs when …? If you were there, would you …? How would you address this problem in life? How can you use this mental model? How can this make a difference? What are the connections? Can I complete this in the time I have?	**4. ANALYSIS: Ability to see parts and relationships** **Matching:** compare and contrast, analogy, metaphor **Classifying:** categorize, sort, group **Analyze Errors:** critique, identify issues, errors in thinking **Generalizing:** create a rule, generalize, draw conclusion **Specifying:** defend, judge, develop an argument for What was important about …? What other ways could ____ be interpreted? What things would you have used to …? What is the main idea of the story (event)? What information supports your explanation? How are these different and alike? Why did the author use this mental model? What are the skills or actions needed?
5. SYNTHESIS: Knowledge utilization **Decision Making:** decide, select, solve, choices **Problem Solving:** see options, overcome obstacles **Experimenting:** generate, test, research, predict **Investigation:** what, why, and how strategies Can you design _____ to show _____? What do you predict will happen if ___ changes? Can you describe events that might occur if …? Pretend you are … What will your future picture look like? What would the world be like if …? How will you use ___ to persuade or convince …? How can humor be used as a resilience strategy? How could the situation have been avoided?	**6. EVALUATION: Judgment based on criteria** **Decision Making:** select best, adapt, solve, figure out **Problem Solving:** use options to reach goal **Experimenting:** generate, test, research, predict **Investigation:** what, why, and how strategies How could you tell if your analysis is reasonable? Would you recommend this ___ to a friend? Why? What do you think will happen to _____? Why? What is the significance of this event in the global perspective or economy? National perspective? What is most compelling to you in this ___? Why? Do you feel _____ is ethical? Why or why not? How will you defend or justify your answer? How will you know it worked?

From K. Dixon on question making, adapted from *Designing and Assessing Educational Objectives*, Marzano and Kendall; *Bloom's Taxonomy*, Bloom, Englehart, Furst, Hill, and Krathwohl; and *A Framework for Understanding Poverty*, Payne. Used with permission.

VII. Reframe Learning Styles

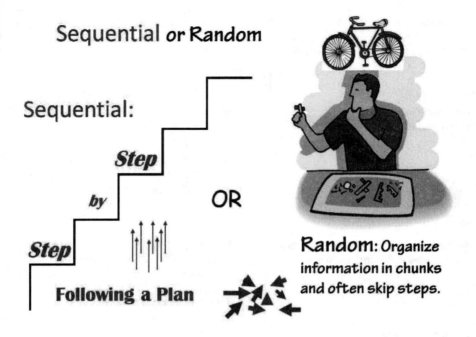

BIG PICTURE or STEP by STEP?

When you start a class or project, do you use the ...

    "Big Picture," the overview or learning objective,
              OR
    Details, individual assignments, steps, etc.,
              OR
    Both?

Learning Styles
How does your learning style compare to your instructor's teaching style?

VIII. Reframe Response

A.   If you choose
        Then you have chosen

        If you choose
        Then you have chosen

B. The Four-Step Reframe

   1. What did you do?

   2. When you did that, what did you want?

   3. What were four things you could have done instead?

   4. What will you do next time?

        C. Reflect

        Write the event or topic.

          1. What are the key points?
            ➢
            ➢
            ➢
            ➢

          2. One insight, thought, or takeaway ...

          3. How does this apply to me and to my life?

          4. Concerns

IX. R Rules Raffiti

IX. Reframe

1. Benny Barnes
2. Mental Models
3. Organizers and Charts
4. Reframe for School and Work
5. Question Making
6. Reading Reframes
7. Learning Styles
8. Reframes for Response
9. Raffiti, Reflect, Resources

4.0	I understand the chapter and can teach the concepts I learned to others. What I learned is important and can be used in the following ways:
3.0	I understand the chapter and do not have any questions about the concepts. What I learned is important because:
2.0	I understand parts of this chapter. I still don't understand and have questions about:
1.0	I still need help to understand the basic concepts of this chapter. Specifically about:
How I will use what I learned in this chapter:	

Rubric by K. Dixon

IX. Reframe Definitions, Symbols, Mental Models, Tools

Definitions

Symbols and Mental Models

Chapter 11 Road Ready—Learning Objectives

What?	Why?	How?
I. Wall of Hope	Use as a mental model of achievements, motivation, and future pictures.	Create and use wall to inspire, motivate, celebrate, and recognize achievements.
II. Work	Understand the importance of service as "work." Develop community and leadership projects.	Discuss work as service and explore personal interests. Create and use project logs for professional portfolios.
III. The Shoulders We Stand On	Understand and identify individuals and historical events that have contributed to and benefited your community.	Identify and present on individuals in your community who have made contributions that have benefited others.
IV. Intellectual Capital	Understand intellectual capital and why it is important.	Define, discuss, and identify strategies to develop intellectual capital.
V. Board of Directors	Understand board of directors in the workplace, as a mental model, and as a personal resource.	Define, discuss, and develop a personal board of directors. Use to develop resources.
VI. Speakers Bureau	Guest speakers inspire, motivate, and inform.	Develop, manage, and use a speakers bureau.
VII. Location	Understand factors, benefits, and choices of locations to live, attend school, and work.	Identify criteria, check future pictures, determine personal options, and plan.
VIII. A Reality	Understand systems, options, and resources for youth.	Create a plan for an individual in foster care. Reframe plans.
IX. Positive Self-Talk	Review and discuss the importance of self-talk.	Review and further develop self-talk.
X. Resource Check	Review resources using R Rules Personal Planners and R Rules Professional Portfolios.	Review resources and revise plans as needed.
XI. Leadership	Review text and information on leadership.	Read about, research, and discuss resources for leadership and personal plans.
XII. The Elephant	Understand and use elephant as a mental model; see different points of view and the importance of working together.	Read and discuss Saxe poem. Discuss different points of view and working together to make a difference.
XIII. The Bigger Picture	Understanding role as citizen and in global community.	Identify role, responsibility, and options to contribute.
Check items to be filed in your R Rules Personal Planner.		

Chapter 11—Road Ready

I. Create a Wall of Hope

Things you would like to give others
Future pictures
Pictures of your "work"
Dreams that have come true
Changes in your community
Accomplishments
Your inventions
Your discoveries
What you will build
What you will lead
A business you will own
Recognition
Celebrations
Video, quotes, photos that inspire

"All men dream: but not equally.
Those who dream by night
in the dusty recesses of their mind
wake in the morning to find that it was vanity;
but the dreamers of the day are dangerous men,
for they may act their dreams with open eyes,
to make it possible."
–T. E. Lawrence

II. Work

In *The R Rules* "work"
is the term for service.

"Service is the rent we pay for living on this earth."
—Shirley Chisholm

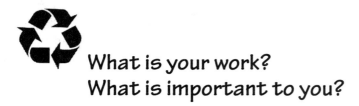 What is your work?
What is important to you?

Learners and Leaders
Leadership and Community Projects

Date	Project	Hours

II. Work

Peach's Neet Feet   https://peachsneetfeet.com/

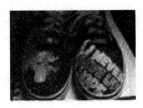

Rachel's Challenge   http://www.rachelschallenge.org/
"I have this theory that if one person can go out of their way to show compassion, then it will start a chain reaction of the same.
People will never know how far a little kindness can go."
            –Rachel Scott

Start a Chain Reaction

"Pay It Forward"

Community Resource Project

Reading Strategies
Bethanie Tucker

Upcycle Store

Lickety Split Chocolate
https://www.youtube.com/watch?v=wjAIL6z4rxc

III. The Shoulders We Stand On

 We all stand on the shoulders of those who came before us.

Identify an individual in your community and
the positive difference
their contributions have made.

1. Develop and deliver a presentation to your class on an individual in your community who has made a positive difference.

2. The format of your presentation is your choice. Examples: a slide presentation, a story board, a recorded interview, a written report or story, or hosting the individual as a guest speaker in your class.

3. Include in your presentation:
   - the individual's contributions
   - a timeline of the individual's life and work in relation to their contributions
   - what difference you feel the individual made
   - how you feel their work has benefited you and others

What is relevant to you?
What contributions have you made?
What contributions will you make?

IV. Intellectual Capital

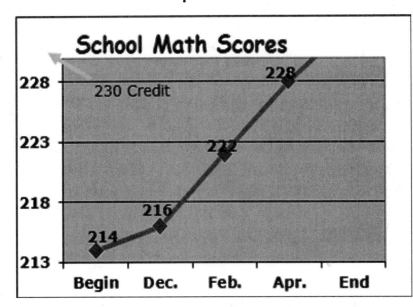

21st Century DOW
The Data On the Wall

21st Century Skills

1. Digital Age Literacy
  Basic Science, Economic, and Technological Literacy
  Visual and Information Literacy
  Multicultural Literacy and Global Awareness

2. Inventive Thinking—Intellectual Capital
  Adaptability, Managing Complexity, and Self-Direction
  Curiosity, Creativity, and Risk Taking
  Higher Order Thinking and Sound Reasoning

3. Interactive Communication—Social and Personal Skills
  Teaming, Collaboration, and Interpersonal Skills
  Personal, Social, and Civic Responsibility
  Interactive Communication

4. Quality, State-of-the-Art Results
  Prioritizing, Planning, and Managing for Results
  Effective Use of Real-World Tools
  Ability to Produce Relevant, High-Quality Products
  http://www.learningpt.org/

The ability to sign the front and the back of a paycheck.

V. Board of Directors

A board of directors is a group of individuals who meet regularly and work together to oversee, inform, and guide the activities of a company or organization.

They have experiences, share knowledge, and are trusted and chosen to help the company make decisions that best support their mission and goals.

Individuals can have a board of directors too. Members of your board may be people you actually know, people you have observed, or people you have only read about.

Who will sit on your board of directors?
Select 5–7 people.
Study and learn from them.

VI. Create and Manage a Speakers Bureau

Inviting guest speakers to your class is a way to learn from others and build bridging capital. Speakers share information about themselves, their experiences and expertise, their jobs and careers, as well as current and historical information about your community.

Once you have buy-in from your group ...
Create an action plan; it might look something like this ...

1. Explore your school's policies and protocol for having guest speakers on campus.
2. Establish a process for requesting speakers.
3. After the process is approved, communicate information and process in writing to members of your organization.
4. Begin building a directory of speakers and the topics and resources they can provide.
5. Designate one person as a point of contact for speakers.

Then use what you have learned in *The R Rules* to work together to develop and manage a speakers bureau for your school or group. Complete the next steps with what you have learned.

6.
7.

VII. Location
   If you could live anywhere in the United States...

Where would you live?
Why?
Top 10 reasons...

VIII. A Reality

John lives in foster care.
When he is 18, he will "age out."
John is 14 now.
Develop a plan for John that will allow him to:
- be independent
- build resources
- be resilient
- reach his future picture

Review your plan.
Review your plan B.
Review R Rules Professional Portfolio.

Chapter 11—Road Ready

IX. Positive Self-Talk
The Language of Resilience

I Promise Myself ...

To stay strong.

To respect myself and others.

To use my resources and talents to make a difference.

To look for possibilities and see options.

To work to make my dreams come true.

To forget the mistakes of the past.

To press on to the accomplishments of my future.

To smile and find humor.

To listen to stories different than my own.

To control the things I can.

To forgive myself for the things I cannot.

To care.

To choose my own way and use my unique voice.

To remember I can.

To hope.

To dream.

To ...

X. Resource Check

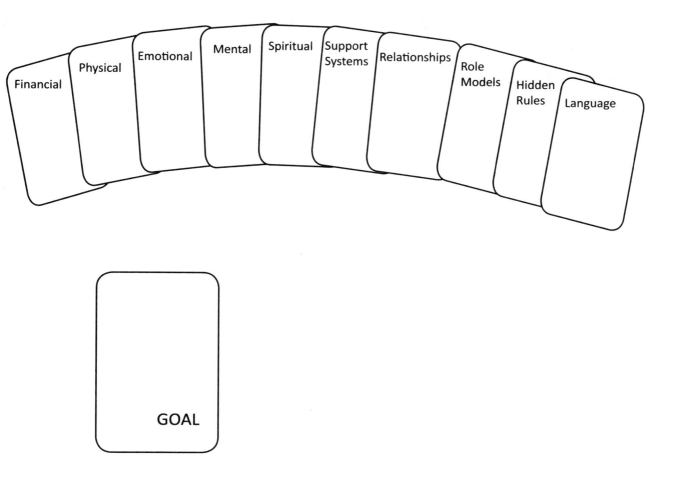

"Young men and women, study yourselves.
See who you really want to be,
and as soon as you see it, say it.
Put it out into the universe.
You must say it and then
go about the business of becoming it."
—Maya Angelou

XI. Leadership

John C. Maxwell's *21 Irrefutable Laws of Leadership*
The Law of the Lid
The Law of Process
The Law of E. F. Hutton
The Law of the Inner Circle
The Law of Empowerment

Seven Grandfather Teachings
https://sites.google.com/a/misd.k12.wi.us/early-college/schools/mihs/oskineniew

>Wisdom
>Love
>Respect
>Bravery
>Honesty
>Humility
>Trust

> "Let us put our heads together and see
> what life we will make for our children."
> –Tatanka Iyotake, Chief of the Lakota Nation

Max DePree, in his book *Leadership Is an Art,* says every great pitcher needs a great catcher. He says, "Any concept of work rises from an understanding of the relationship between pitchers and catchers."

XI. Leadership

I Believe
John D. Rockefeller

"I believe in the supreme worth of the individual and in his right to life, liberty, and the pursuit of happiness.

I believe that every right implies a responsibility; every opportunity, an obligation; every possession, a duty.

I believe that the law was made for man and not man for the law; that government is the servant of the people and not their master.

I believe in the dignity of labor, whether with head or hand; that the world owes no man a living but that it owes every man an opportunity to make a living.

I believe in the sacredness of a promise, that a man's word should be as good as his bond, that character—not wealth or power or position—is of supreme worth.

I believe that love is the greatest thing in the world; that it alone can overcome hate; that right can and will triumph over might."

What do you believe?
Write your belief statement.

I Believe ...

XII. The Elephant

Six blind men of Indostan sought to learn about the elephant.

The first man leaned against the side of the elephant
    and told the others the elephant was like a huge wall.
The second man felt the elephant's tusk and declared
    the elephant was like a spear, round and smooth and sharp.
The third man, holding the elephant's squirming trunk,
    understood the elephant was like a snake.
The fourth, holding on to the giant animal's knee,
    thought the elephant was most like a tree.
The fifth, holding the elephant's flopping ear,
    knew the elephant was like a giant fan.
The sixth, holding the elephant's swinging tail,
    said the elephant was a rope.

Each man used his own experience and argued about the elephant.
    –Adapted from "The Blind Men and
    the Elephant" by John Godfrey Saxe.

"The elephant in the room" is a term for realities that are often being ignored or overlooked. The term is also used to describe a difficult situation or truth that is obvious but not discussed or addressed. Today in the United States, "elephants" roam the halls of our schools and the streets of our communities.

We each have unique talents and strengths. We each have different points of view and realities. Like the blind men in Saxe's poem, we can use our own realities, or we can work together to build the future pictures—for ourselves and our communities—that we want to live in. Use *The R Rules* to build resources, listen, and lead.

Your mind is a weapon, a tool, and a resource.

XIII. What are you a part of?
The bigger picture ...

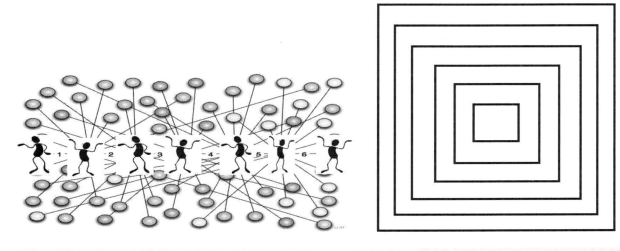

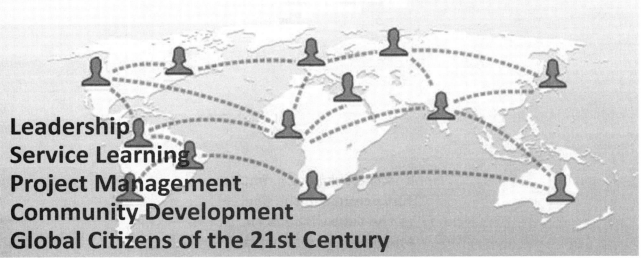

www.freerice.com
www.heifer.org/gift

Civic Organizations
Clubs and Teams
Service Organizations
Community Projects
Boards and Councils
Local Government
Workforce

"'Hope' is the thing with feathers—
That perches in the soul—
And sings the tune without the words—
And never stops—at all."
–Emily Dickinson

Appendix

Date Entered	To Do/Document	Date Completed

Date Entered	To Do/Document	Date Completed

Date Entered	To Do/Document	Date Completed

Date Entered	To Do/Document	Date Completed

Date Entered	To Do/Document	Date Completed

Date Entered	To Do/Document	Date Completed

Date Entered	To Do/Document	Date Completed

Date Entered	To Do/Document	Date Completed

Plan Backwards

	1 2 3 4 5 6 7
	1 2 3 4 5 6 7
	1 2 3 4 5 6 7
	1 2 3 4 5 6 7
	1 2 3 4 5 6 7
	1 2 3 4 5 6 7
	1 2 3 4 5 6 7

1	
2	
3	
4	
5	
6	
7	
8	
9	
10	

Name _____

Technology

	0	.5	1	1.5	2	2.5	3	3.5	4	
										Using a variety of technological tools to gather and distribute information
										Using technology to create and enhance projects in a variety of situations
										Using technology to research, expand, and apply new knowledge
										Demonstrating student social responsibility
										Demonstrating global awareness and competence
										Vocabulary: global awareness, student social responsibility

R^U Progress Check developed by K. Dixon and B. Souther.

Name _____

Participation									
0	.5	1	1.5	2	2.5	3	3.5	4	
									Contributing to classroom discussions with ideas and positive effort
									Listening respectfully
									Asking for clarification when needed
									Self-evaluating individual roles in the classroom
									Maintaining appropriate attendance
									Using and maintaining R Rules Personal Planner
									Vocabulary: role, respectfully

R^U Progress Check developed by K. Dixon and B. Souther.

Name _____

Behavior									
	0	.5	1	1.5	2	2.5	3	3.5	4
Following directions									
Following classroom and school rules									
Demonstrating respect for self, others, and property									
Accepting responsibility for own actions									

Vocabulary: respect, responsibility

R^U Progress Check developed by K. Dixon and B. Souther.

Name_____

	0	.5	1	1.5	2	2.5	3	3.5	4			

R^U Progress Check developed by K. Dixon and B. Souther.

Name_____

	0	.5	1	1.5	2	2.5	3	3.5	4

R^U Progress Check developed by K. Dixon and B. Souther.

Bibliography

ACT. (2006). ACT workkeys. Iowa City, IA: ACT. Retrieved from http://www.act.org/products/workforce-act-workkeys/

American School Counselor Association. (2004). *The ASCA national model workbook: A companion guide to implementing a comprehensive school counseling program.* Alexandria, VA: ASCA.

Andrews, A. (2006). Keynote address at the New Mexico Public Education All Kids Conference. Hyatt Regency Tamaya. Bernalillo, New Mexico, June 1.

Bandler, R., & Grinder, J. (1979). *Frogs into princes.* Moab, UT: Real People Press.

Berne, E. (1996). *Games people play: The psychology of human relationships.* New York, NY: Grove Press.

Bloom, B. (ed.). (1984). *Taxonomy of educational objectives: Handbook 1: Cognitive domain* (2nd ed.). New York, NY: Longman.

Bowers, J., & Hatch, T. (2003). *The ASCA national model: A framework for school counseling programs.* Alexandria, VA: ASCA.

Brazee, E., & Burkhardt, R. (1997). *Choices and consequences curriculum.* New York, NY: Courtroom Television Network.

Breaking ranks: Changing an American institution. (1996). Reston, VA: National Association of Secondary School Principals.

Brown, G. (1998). Quality in the classroom: Strengthening quality in schools. Paper presented at Energy Training Center, Kirtland Air Force Base, Albuquerque, NM, April 14.

Bruett, K. (2006). Real and relevant 21st century skills. *Converge, 1*(1), 60–65.

BYU Native American Programs (Producer). (2008). *Voices of leadership* [DVD]. Provo, UT: Brigham Young University.

Carroll, L. (1984). *Alice's adventures in wonderland and through the looking-glass.* New York, NY: Bantam Classics.

Center for New American Media (Producer), & Alvarez, L., & Kolker, A. (Directors). (2001). *People like us: Social class in America* [TV movie]. USA: WETA and Center for New American Media.

Clark, R. (2003). *The essential 55.* New York, NY: Hyperion.

Comer, J. (2005). Keynote address at the Association for Supervision and Curriculum Development conference, San Francisco Marriott, San Francisco, CA, October 24.

Common Core State Standards Initiative home page. (2015). Retrieved from http://www.corestandards.org/

Covey, S. (1989). *The 7 habits of highly effective people: Powerful lessons in personal change.* New York, NY: Simon & Schuster.

Covey, S. (1998). *The 7 habits of highly effective teens.* New York, NY: Simon & Schuster.

Covey, S. (2004). *The 8th habit: From effectiveness to greatness.* New York, NY: Simon & Schuster.

Cox, T. (Producer), & Haines, R. (Director). (2006). *The Ron Clark story* [TV movie]. Canada: The Alberta Film Development Program of the Alberta Foundation for the Arts.

Crockett, L., Jukes, I., & Churches, A. (2012, February). 21st century fluencies for the digital age. *Middle Ground,* 9–11. Retrieved from https://promiseroad.files.wordpress.com/2012/03/21st-century-fluencies-for-the-digital-age.pdf

Daggett, W. (2003). Rigor and relevance. Paper given at the Quality in Education Conference, Hyatt Regency, Albuquerque, NM, September 23.

Darendou, Y., Lioud, C., & Priou, E. (Producers), & Jacquet, L. (Director). (2005). *March of the penguins* [Motion picture]. France: Bonne Pioche.

Deming, W. E. (1982). *Out of the crisis.* Cambridge, MA: MIT Press.

DePree, M. (1989). *Leadership is an art.* New York, NY: Dell.

Develop a career ladder/lattice. (2015). Competency Model Clearinghouse. Retrieved from http://www.careeronestop.org/CompetencyModel/userguide_cll.aspx

DeVol, P. E. (2006). *Getting ahead in a just-gettin'-by world: Building your resources for a better life* (2nd rev. ed.). Highlands, TX: aha! Process.

DeVol, P. E. (2014). 12 thinking tools for Bridges Out of Poverty initiatives. aha! Process. Retrieved from http://www.ahaprocess.com/wp-content/uploads/2014/04/12-Thinking-Tools-for-Bridges-Initiatives.pdf

Dixon, K. (2010). Moving forward. Staff development presentation, Farmington Municipal Schools, Farmington, NM.

Drucker, P. (1992). *Managing for the future: The 1990s and beyond.* New York, NY: Truman Talley.

DuFour, R., DuFour, R., Eaker, R., & Karhanek, G. (2004). *Whatever it takes: How professional learning communities respond when kids don't learn.* Bloomington, IN: Solution Tree.

Dusa, G. (2000). *Practical activities for achieving success with difficult and at-risk students.* Madison, WI: National At-Risk Education Network.

Eaker, R. (2006). Presentation to educators given at the 20th Street Conference Center, Farmington, NM, November 30.

Eaker, R., DuFour, R., & DuFour, R. (2002). *Getting started: Reculturing schools to become professional learning communities.* Bloomington, IN: National Educational Service.

East, G. (1997). Rules without relationships breed rebellion. *Texas Study of Secondary Education, 6*(2), 12–14, 25.

Ellis, K. D. (2004). *Putting the pieces together.* Highlands, TX: aha! Process, Inc.

Ellis, K. D. (2007). *Cookin' in the classroom!* Highlands, TX: aha! Process, Inc.

Emerald, D. (2010). *The power of TED: The empowerment dynamic.* Bainbridge Island, WA: Polaris.

Exploring opportunity: A high school student's guide to college. (2003). Santa Fe, NM: New Mexico Commission on Higher Education.

Farr, J. L., & York, C. M. (1975). Amount of information and primacy-recency effects in recruitment decisions. *Personnel Psychology, 28,* 233–238. doi: 10.1111/j.1744-6570.1975.tb01383.x

Fralick, M., Aguilar, B. Z., & Gauthier, L. (2012). *Native American college and career success.* Dubuque, IA: Kendall Hunt.

Feuerstein, R. (with Rand, Y, Hoffman, M. B., & Miller, R.). (1980). *Instrumental enrichment: An intervention program for cognitive modifiability.* Glenview, IL: Scott, Foresman.

Frankl, V. (1959). *Man's search for meaning.* Boston, MA: Beacon Press.

Fried, R. N., & Woods, C. (Producers), & Anspaugh, D. (Director). (1993). *Rudy.* USA: TriStar Pictures.

Gandhi, A. (2000, spring). Reflections of peace. *Brigham Young University Magazine.* Retrieved from http://magazine.byu.edu/?act=view&a=152.

Garrison, W. (1992). *Why you say it.* Nashville, IN: Rutledge Hill.

Gladwell, M. (2005). *Blink: The power of thinking without thinking.* New York, NY: Time Warner.

Gladwell, M. (2008). *Outliers: The story of success.* New York, NY: Hachette.

Goleman, D. (1998). *Working with emotional intelligence.* New York, NY: Bantam Books.

Gruwell, E. (1999). *The freedom writers diary.* New York, NY: Broadway.

Hanson, L. (2003). *Poverty project.* St. Paul, MN: Good Ground.

Hart, B., & Risley, T. (1999). *Meaningful differences in the everyday experience of young American children.* Baltimore, MD: Paul H. Brookes.

Henry, A., & Milstein, M. (2001). Helping school leaders build strong relationships with their communities using resiliency strategies. Paper presented to the New Mexico Coalition for School Administrators, Hyatt Regency Hotel, Albuquerque, NM, July 23.

ICOMOS International Cultural Tourism Charter. (2002). *Principles and guidelines for managing tourism at places of cultural and heritage significance.* New York, NY: ICOMOS International Cultural Tourism Committee.

Jackson, T. (1993). *Activities that teach.* Telluride, CO: Red Rock.

Jalongo, M. R. (1991). *Creating learning communities: The role of the teacher in the 21st century.* Bloomington, IN: National Education Service.

Jenkins, L. (2004). *Permission to forget: And nine other root causes of America's frustration with education.* Milwaukee, WI: American Society for Quality.

Jensen, E. (2009). *Teaching with poverty in mind: What being poor does to kids' brains and what schools can do about it.* Alexandria, VA. Association for Supervision and Curriculum Development.

Joos, M. (1967). *The five clocks: A linguistic excursion into the five styles of English usage.* New York, NY: Harcourt, Brace, and World.

Jordan, M. (1994). *I can't accept not trying: Michael Jordan on the pursuit of excellence.* New York, NY: HarperCollins.

Karpman, S. (1968). Fairy tales and script drama analysis. *Transactional Analysis Bulletin, 7*(26), 39–43.

Khan Academy home page. (2015). Khan Academy. Retrieved from https://www.khanacademy.org/

Kuhn, T. (1962). *The structure of scientific revolutions.* Chicago, IL: University of Chicago Press.

Kuiper, K. (Ed.). (1995). *Merriam-Webster's encyclopedia of literature.* Springfield, MA: Merriam-Webster.

Lawrence, T. E. (2011). *Seven pillars of wisdom: A triumph.* Blacksburg, VA: Wilder.

Lemke, C. (2002). enGauge 21st century skills: Digital literacies for a digital age. ED463753. Retrieved from http://files.eric.ed.gov/fulltext/ED463753.pdf

Levine, M. (2002). *A mind at a time.* New York, NY: Simon & Schuster.

Levitt, S., & Dubner, S. (2005). *Freakonomics.* New York, NY: William Morrow.

Lucas, T. R. (2003). Presentation at Schools That Learn conference, Marriott Manhattan, New York, NY, July 1.

Macklin, J. W. (2004). Extemporaneous comments at *The 8th habit* book release, Snowbird Resort, Park City, UT, November 4.

Martignoni, M. E. (Ed.). (1955). *Illustrated treasury of children's literature.* New York, NY: Grosset and Dunlap.

Marzano, R. J. (1992). *A different kind of classroom: Teaching with dimensions of learning.* Alexandria, VA: Association for Supervision and Curriculum Development.

Marzano, R. J. (2003a). *School leadership that works: From research to results.* Alexandria, VA: Association for Supervision and Curriculum Development.

Marzano, R. J. (2003b). *What works in schools: Translating research into action.* Alexandria, VA: Association for Supervision and Curriculum Development.

Marzano, R. J. (2004). *Building background knowledge for academic achievement.* Alexandria, VA: Association for Supervision and Curriculum Development.

Marzano, R. J. (2007). *The art and science of teaching.* Alexandria, VA: Association for Supervision and Curriculum Development.

Marzano, R. J., & Kendall, J. S. (2007). *The new taxonomy of educational objectives.* Thousand Oaks, CA: Corwin Press.

Marzano, R. J., & Kendall, J. S. (2008). *Designing and assessing educational objectives applying the new taxonomy.* Thousand Oaks, CA: Corwin Press.

Marzano, R. J., Norford, J. S., Paynter, D. E., Pickering, D. J., & Gaddy, B. B. (2004). *A handbook for classroom instruction that works.* Alexandria, VA: Association for Supervision and Curriculum Development.

Marzano, R. J., & Pickering, D. (2005). *Building academic vocabulary: Teacher's manual.* Alexandria, VA: Association for Supervision and Curriculum Development.

Marzano, R. J., Pickering, D., & Pollock, J. (2001). *Classroom instruction that works: Research-based strategies for increasing student achievement.* Alexandria, VA: Association for Supervision and Curriculum Development.

Maugham, W. S. (2003). *The razor's edge.* New York, NY: Vintage Books.

Maxwell, J. C. (1998). *The 21 irrefutable laws of leadership.* Nashville, TN: Thomas Nelson.

Maxwell, J. C. (2001). *Developing the leader within you.* Nashville, TN: Thomas Nelson.

McBride, W. (1997). *Entertaining an elephant.* San Francisco, CA: Pearl Street Press.

McClanahan, E., & Wicks, C. (1993). *Future force: Kids that want to, can, and do!* Chino Hills, CA: PACT.

Miller, S. C. (2008). *Until it's gone: Ending poverty in our nation, in our lifetime.* Highlands, TX: aha! Process.

Mitchell, W. (2002). *It's not what happens to you, it's what you do about it* [DVD]. Arvada, CO: W Mitchell.

Montaño-Harmon, M. R. (1991). Discourse features of written Mexican Spanish: Current research in contrastive rhetoric and its implications. *Hispania, 74*(2), 417–425.

Morrison, T. (1999). *The big box.* New York, NY: Hyperion.

National Association of State Directors of Career Technical Education Consortium. (2015). Career clusters. Retrieved from http://www.careertech.org/career-clusters

National Career Development Association. (2015). Guidelines. Retrieved from http://www.ncda.org/aws/NCDA/pt/sp/guidelines

O'Banion, T. (1997). *A learning college for the 21st century.* Phoenix, AZ: American Council on Education/Oryx Press.

O'Neil, J. (1995). On schools as learning organizations: A conversation with Peter Senge. *Educational Leadership, 52*(7), 20–23.

Oprah's debt diet action plan. (2015). Retrieved from http://www.oprah.com/money/Debt-Relief-from-Oprahs-Debt-Diet-Action-Plan.

Oskineniew kenaepuahkam. (n.d.) Menominee Early College Model. Retrieved from https://sites.google.com/a/misd.k12.wi.us/early-college/schools/mihs/oskineniew

Parella, J. (1990). *The main stalk: A synthesis of Navajo philosophy.* Tucson, AZ: University of Arizona.

Patterson, K., Grenny, J., McMillan, R., & Switzler, A. (2002). *Crucial conversations: Tools for talking when stakes are high.* New York, NY: McGraw Hill.

Payne, R. K. (1999). *Preventing school violence by creating emotional safety.* Highlands, TX: aha! Process.

Payne, R. K. (2002). *Understanding learning: The how, the why, and the what.* Highlands, TX: aha! Process.

Payne, R. K. (2005a). *Crossing the tracks for love.* Highlands, TX: aha! Process.

Payne, R. K. (2005b). *Learning structures* (3rd rev. ed.). Highlands, TX: aha! Process.

Payne, R. K. (2013). *A framework for understanding poverty* (5th rev. ed.). Highlands, TX: aha! Process.

Payne, R. K., DeVol, P. E., & Dreussi-Smith, T. (2009). *Bridges out of poverty: Strategies for professionals and communities* (3rd rev. ed.). Highlands, TX: aha! Process.

Payne, R. K., & Krabill, D. (2002). *Hidden rules of class at work.* Highlands, TX: aha! Process.

Payne, R. K., & Magee, D. (2001). *Meeting standards and raising test scores: When you don't have much time or money* (Rev. ed.). Highlands, TX: aha! Process.

Paynter, D. (2008). Strengthening vocabulary. Presentation for Farmington Municipal School District, Farmington, NM.

Paynter, D., Bodrova, E., & Doty, J. (2005). *For the love of words.* San Francisco, CA: Jossey-Bass.

Peregoy, J. (2002). Presentation at Quality New Mexico Conference, Old Town Sheraton, Albuquerque, NM, March 8.

Pfarr, J. (2006). *Jodi's stories* [DVD]. Highlands, TX: aha! Process.

Pfarr, J. (2009). *Tactical communication.* Highlands, TX: aha! Process.

Pierson, R. (2003). *Rita's stories* [DVD]. Highlands, TX: aha! Process.

Practical Money Skills for Life home page. (2015). Retrieved from http://practicalmoneyskills.com

Prickett, T. J., Gada-Jain, N., & Bernieri, F. (2000). *The importance of first impressions in a job interview.* Paper presented at the annual meeting of the Midwestern Psychological Association, Chicago, IL, May.

Rapke, J., Starkey, S., & Zemeckis, R. (Producers), & Anderson, J. (Director). (2005). *The prize winner of Defiance, Ohio* [Motion picture]. USA: DreamWorks.

Reed, J. (2007, November 30). Lost generation [video]. YouTube. Retrieved from https://www.youtube.com/watch?v=42E2fAWM6rA

Reeves, D. (2002). *The daily disciplines of leadership.* San Francisco, CA: Jossey-Bass.

Saxe, J. G. (1878). The blind men and the elephant. In W. J. Linton (ed.), *Poetry of America.* London, England: George Bell and Sons.

Schargel, F. (2003). *Dropout prevention tools.* Larchmont, NY: Eye on Education.

Schargel, F., & Smink, J. (2001). *Strategies to help solve our school dropout problem.* Larchmont, NY: Eye on Education.

Schumacher, M. (2006). Presentation on career clusters, San Juan College, Farmington, NM, April 4.

Senegor, K. M. (2013, September 2). A conversation with Dr. Maya Angelou. *Women for One.* Retrieved from http://womenforone.com/a-conversation-with-dr-maya-angelou/

Senge, P., Cambron-McCabe, N., Lucas, T., Smith, B., Dutton, J., & Kleiner A. (2000). *Schools that learn: A fifth discipline fieldbook for educators, parents, and everyone who cares about education.* New York, NY: Doubleday.

Senge, P., Ross, R., Smith, B., Roberts, C., & Kleiner, A. (1994). *The fifth discipline fieldbook.* New York, NY: Doubleday.

Slocumb, P. (2004). *Hear our cry: Boys in crisis.* Highlands, TX: aha! Process.

Smith, B. (1943). *A tree grows in Brooklyn.* New York, NY: Harper.

Sroka, S. R. (2005). Making a difference with the power of one: The double crib. Keynote address, Association for Supervision and Curriculum Development Conference, San Francisco Marriott, San Francisco, CA, October 24.

Stailey, J., & Payne, R. K. (1998). *Think rather of zebra: Dealing with aspects of poverty through story.* Highlands, TX: aha! Process.

Stafford, W. (1993). A ritual to read to each other. In R. Blyed (ed.), *The darkness around us is deep: Selected poems of William Stafford.* New York, NY: Harper Perennial.

Stay in the groove. (2002). Santa Fe, NM: New Mexico Department of Labor.

Tomlinson, C. A. (1999). *The differentiated classroom: Responding to the needs of all learners.* Alexandria, VA: Association for Supervision and Curriculum Development.

Tough choices tough times: The report of the new commission on the skills of the American workforce. (2007). Washington, DC: National Center on Education and the Economy.

Trilling, B., & Fadel, C. (2012). *21st century skills: Learning for life in our times.* San Francisco, CA: Jossey-Bass.

Tucker, B. H. (2001). *Tucker signing strategies for reading.* Highlands, TX: aha! Process.

Tucker, B. H. (2005). *The journey of Al and Gebra to the land of algebra.* Highlands, TX: aha! Process.

UNESCO. (2014). *Intangible cultural heritage.* Paris, France: UNESCO.

United States Census Bureau. (2013). *Current population survey, 2013 annual social and economic supplement.* Washington, DC: United States Census Bureau.

Wade, C., & Tavris, C. (1999). *Invitation to psychology.* Upper Saddle River, NY: Prentice Hall.

Wage information for job seekers: Northern WIA area. (2007). Santa Fe, NM: New Mexico Department of Labor, Economic Research and Analysis Bureau.

Wagner, T. (2012). *Creating innovators: The making of young people who will change the world.* New York, NY: Scribner.

What work requires of schools: A SCANS report for America. (2000). Prepared by The Secretary's Commission on Achieving Necessary Skills. Washington, DC: United States Department of Labor.

Wheatley, M. (1994). *Leadership and the new science: Learning about organization from an orderly universe.* San Francisco, CA: Berrett-Koehler.

Wicks, C., Peregoy, J., & Wheeler, J. (2001). *Plugged in!* New Bern, NC: Class Action.

Williamson, M. (1992). *A return to love: Reflections on the principles of a course in miracles.* New York, NY: HarperCollins.

Wilson, W. J. (2009). *More than just race: Being black and poor in the inner city.* Washington, DC: Poverty and Race Action Council.

Your job: Will you keep it or lose it? (2001). Santa Fe, NM: New Mexico Department of Labor.